'Jack has given us a gift –
crucial topic that we mus............ .. .a.itastic
mixture of real stories, real warnings and real hope. Read
it!'
*Tim Alford, Director of Limitless, the national youth
department of the Elim Pentecostal Churches*

'Refreshingly honest, clear, inspiring and practical. This
book is a vital contribution to the pursuit of holiness in a
digital age.'
Gavin Calver, Director of Mission for the Evangelical Alliance

A BETTER KIND OF INTIMACY

The Price of Porn and How to Overcome it

JACK SKETT

instant
ap□stle

First published in Great Britain in 2018

Instant Apostle
The Barn
1 Watford House Lane
Watford
Herts
WD17 1BJ

British Library Cataloguing-in-Publication Data

A catalogue record for this book is available from the British Library

This book and all other Instant Apostle books are available from Instant Apostle:

Website: www.instantapostle.com
E-mail: info@instantapostle.com

ISBN 978-1-909728-81-3

Printed in Great Britain

Dedicated to David and Liz Ollerton, whose example of life and faith continues to inspire me, and who provided valuable notes on this book even while David underwent chemotherapy. David has truly been promoted to glory.

'Well done, good and faithful servant.'
(Matthew 25:21)

Acknowledgements

This book has been a journey for me – one which I have not travelled alone. My most important acknowledgement and thanks go to God, who loved me even when I was trying to find my fulfilment in porn instead of Him. He rescued me from that life and set me on this path. All glory to Him.

My wife, Annie, has been a constant encouragement to me during this process. Along the way she also gave birth to our son Josiah David, who has made quite an impression already.

The team at Instant Apostle have worked hard with me to make this book a reality. Thank you particularly to Manoj for welcoming me into the IA family. Thanks as well to Sheila, my editor – you were ruthless in the right places; your edits and advice have made this a better book than it would have been!

Tamara Cameron, you didn't know it, but several chapters of this book were written in your coffee shop. Thank you for the lattes!

Thank you to Iain and the elders at Elim Church Selly Oak. I'm excited by the adventure we're on with Jesus!

Contents

Introduction

24th August, AD 79. The people of Pompeii had just finished celebrating Vulcanalia, the festival of the Roman god of fire. Nature, it seems, is not without a sense of irony. Only a day after the Vulcanalia celebrations, the great volcano Vesuvius erupted, obliterating Pompeii and several other towns nearby. Pompeii was entirely buried in rubble, and forgotten for more than 1,000 years.

After its first rediscovery in 1599, various archaeologists searched in Pompeii to discover more about this forgotten city and its culture. In 1863, Giuseppe Fiorelli led an excavation which uncovered several erotic artworks, which were abruptly hidden away out of embarrassment. Among the artworks were sculptures and drawings of Priapus, the Roman god of sex and fertility, as well as depictions of sexual acts which have been interpreted as options for services provided in Pompeii's brothels. This discovery is one of the pieces of evidence by which people claim that prostitution is the oldest profession in the world.

Whether or not this particular claim is true, history is clear that humankind's sexual desire has been both a blessing and a curse for as long can be remembered. It was

Paris' sexual desire for Helen which brought about the destruction of Troy when her husband sought revenge. Israel's King David almost derailed his entire kingdom because of his lust for Bathsheba, and his son Solomon oversaw the beginning of the kingdom's decline largely because of his misplaced sexual desire (he had 700 wives and 300 concubines!).

Sexual desire is a trait shared by all people. By some it is considered to be a snare from which one should flee, and by others a normal part of life which should be embraced in whatever context one chooses. Both of these viewpoints can, in their own way, lead to someone using pornography.

The problem is that both of these views of sexuality are flawed, and yet they appear to dominate a lot of debate on the subject. If we're urged to avoid and suppress our sexual desire entirely, we're missing out on an incredible gift from God, which He intended for us to enjoy. By the same token, if we embrace it on a whim, giving in to our desires fully and exercising our sexuality without any restraint, we're misusing sex and tainting the wonderful God-given gift that it is.

Our society teaches us that if something *feels* good, it must *be* good, and therefore we are entitled to it. Yet, we are aware that too much of a good thing can be bad for us, and that some things which feel good in the moment have incredibly harmful effects.

It is something of a rarity today to meet someone whose life has not been touched in some way by pornography. Perhaps you're one of those fortunate people, and you're reading this in order to understand what so many people go through in this regard. You might have come into contact with porn just briefly and it holds no power over you. You may even be someone who has previously struggled or is currently struggling with addiction to pornography. My hope is that, whichever of these categories you fall into, you will find this book helpful.

This is a book about porn. Of course, porn is about sex, so in essence this is a book about sex. Christians are not generally accustomed to talking about sex. We tend to be too uncomfortable and embarrassed to talk about it with one another, and it is not often taught about in the context of a sermon. We need to fight past our discomfort and engage in conversation about sex, because that's what people outside the Church are doing.

Pornography may never be completely eradicated from our society, but I believe that its hold over the lives of individuals can be broken by the power of God. For our part, we can seek to attain a healthy view of sex, in order to better understand why God created it and therefore why pornography distorts it. We need to rediscover the gift of intimacy – something pornography promises, but fails to reproduce. I write this from experience, as a 'survivor'. It makes sense, then, to begin with my story.

1
Porn and Me

This is a very important book for me to write. Porn is a very serious problem in our society today, and I'm passionate about seeing men and women freed from addiction to it. However, that's only the first reason for its importance. This second reason is a very personal one. Here, then, is my story.

I had the great privilege of being raised in a Christian home. We went to an Anglican church as a family, where I was taught from the Bible in Sunday school. I learned the Ten Commandments, was familiar with the life of Jesus and had a good knowledge of Old Testament stories. Sadly for me I never learned how to apply these things to my life, or even that it was important to do so. Mine was an all too common type of Christianity. I would go to church every Sunday, but it made very little difference to the way I lived my life throughout the rest of the week. Every year my family and I would go to a Christian festival and I would meet with God in a powerful way. I would come home excited about God, determined to live for Him, and yet within a couple of weeks I'd be back to how I was before.

When I was about fourteen I had my first experience with online pornography. (My first encounter with any form of porn was years earlier, though, when I was eight years old and my friend brought a playing card with a picture of a naked woman into school and showed me.) The initial contact came from a visit to a friend's house after school one day. We spent a couple of hours playing a wrestling game on his PlayStation before we got bored. He decided that it'd be fun to look at some porn websites. I admit that I didn't even fully know what that meant at that point! I'd never seen anything like the images that were suddenly before my eyes. It felt both wrong and exciting at the same time, although to a young teenage boy I think the exciting part outweighed the wrongness of it.

A few days later I decided to explore further for myself. My family was out for the evening and I was talking to one of my friends online.[1] I asked him if he knew any good websites I could look at, and he sent me a link. From there I was hooked, and every opportunity I had when my family were out I would log on, exploring further and further in this new world. I couldn't help myself, I just had to see more, and so I kept looking. It got to a point where I would even look at porn when my family were in. It'd be mostly late at night when I thought no one would come and find me, but I was willing to risk being caught because I just needed to get a 'fix'. I don't think I realised at that point that I had an addiction, but soon the minimum wasn't enough – it just didn't do it for me any more, so I began to look for more extreme things.

The unimaginable sin

I think a lot of people have a bit of a warped view of pornography. Some see it as an acceptable thing – we're all human after all, we all have sexual urges and what's wrong with indulging them every once in a while? Others see it as filthy – the unimaginable sin which taints the sinner irrevocably, and you mustn't ever speak about it. Still others have a very one-sided view. They focus on the objectification and exploitation of women and condemn the men who watch them. Of course, one of the most damaging things about porn is the effect it has on the actors who take part in it; something I'd never deny or diminish. It is a mistake, however, to assume that this is where the effects stop.

Here's the reality: porn warps the watcher's view of sex, women (or men – this can be an issue for women as well), and of themselves. It promises fulfilment that it can never deliver, so you watch more and more in search of that fulfilment. Eventually you can't help yourself. You know it's wrong and it's ruining you, but you aren't strong enough to quit. Sound familiar? What I've just described looks just like a drug addiction.

That's how it was for me. So many times I promised myself I was going to give up. A few times I even went as far as deleting all the clips I had saved on the computer, but it was never long before I succumbed again. The clearest thing I can compare it to is a smoker who, proclaiming that they're quitting declares, 'This is my last one!'

21

It's never the last one. I lost count of how many 'last ones' I had. I used to pray and promise God that I was going to stop, that I would do it this time. All that ever achieved was that I felt even more guilty. The apostle Paul warns against this attitude in his letter to the Galatians:

> Are you so foolish? After beginning by means of the Spirit, are you now trying to finish by means of the flesh?[2]

Of course, I couldn't talk to anyone about it, because it felt too dirty, too scandalous and too embarrassing. One night my brother caught me, and instead of asking for his help I raged at him. I accused him of judging me and of spying on me. The way I was talking to him, it was as if it was all his fault! I thought he was going to tell our parents, but he never did, and I just tried to hide it better.

That particular encounter shows me how porn had changed my character. I'm normally quite an easy-going person, and I'm certainly not prone to angry outbursts. Again, it comes back to addiction. Addicts can tend to become angry when confronted about their addiction – like the way an animal backed into a corner will lash out in ferocious self-defence. I know that some still perceive porn to be a harmless engagement with your sexual urges. My experience has shown me more than that; it changed me.

'There's something on you'

Years passed and I continued to struggle alone. In 2006 I was seventeen and I went with some friends to a Christian youth camp. At the beginning of that week I decided to quit smoking (I had started less than a year previously) and so I did my best to persevere throughout the week.

In one of the evening sessions I heard a talk which changed everything. I can't even remember the details of what the guy spoke about – it was something to do with twelve-foot-tall angels and I wasn't sure of the theology behind it all. He ended his talk with an appeal for people to come forward for healing from addictions, eating disorders and things of a similar nature. He shouted, 'There's something on you. God can see it, and I can see it!' I was terrified that this man could see what was on me!

One of the effects that porn can have on people is that it can feel like a burden on your shoulders, which seems impossible to lift. I'd been carrying a weight of shame and guilt about my addiction. I'd tried as hard as I could to quit, and failed every time. It felt like there was something really dirty staining me, so for this man to talk about being able to see what was on me was frightening.

I stood up, along with hundreds of others. One of my friends stood up with me and I told him that I wanted prayer for quitting smoking, but in my heart I said to myself and to God that I really wanted to quit porn. Ideally, I should have been honest with my friend as well as with God, but it had taken all the courage I could muster to stand up in the first place. My friend prayed for me and we sat down. The first thing I noticed was that I no longer wanted to smoke, so we all got pretty excited. In that moment I knew that I was free and porn no longer had a hold on me. I was instantly and completely delivered from my addiction. The heavy burden of shame and guilt that

I'd been carrying for all those years was gone. That same night I gave my heart to Jesus in a real and permanent way and determined to serve Him. As I write this, it is now ten years since I last looked at, or had any desire to look at, porn. God is good!

Every journey is different

Let me just clarify something here, because I don't want to accidentally mislead anyone. God blessed me by instantly delivering me from my addiction, but this is not guaranteed. We know that all things are possible for God, but at no point does he promise us an end to all our problems.

I've shared my story with people before, who have revealed to me that they're struggling with porn. A common question that I'm asked then is, 'Will God deliver me like he delivered you?' I find that such a difficult question to answer! I've known people to get frustrated with God then, because they so desperately want to be set free. I've even been on the wrong end of jealousy, because I was set free and they weren't. Thankfully, those experiences are very rare, but I will say that although God did deliver me and I haven't been anywhere near porn since, it doesn't mean that I have it easy. I've already described to you the years I spent trying to fix the problem myself. I've told about the shame I carried alone. I don't think it's ever easy to overcome addiction. I experienced a miracle, after several years of struggle.

The reality is that more often than not God works through a gradual process. This involves pain, but also growth. I've heard people preaching that Jesus will solve all of your problems, or that He will definitely heal you from any and all sickness. This can be a damaging message to preach because it leaves people with a warped idea, not only of who God is but also of who they are. What if God doesn't heal you? Does that mean He doesn't care? Does that mean you aren't good enough, or you don't have enough faith? I don't think so.

The apostle Paul tells us that 'in all things God works for the good of those who love him'.[3] So, if you love God you can trust that, no matter what the situation, He is on your side. The important thing is to continue to trust God and seek His help, whether that turns out to be through a healing or deliverance in a moment or the Holy Spirit giving you strength to persevere through a long recovery process.

Although I was set free from my addiction, I still feel that it's necessary to protect myself. After all, an alcoholic doesn't go back to drinking, even in moderation, in case they fall back into old habits. The book of Proverbs says, 'Above all else, guard your heart, for everything you do flows from it.'[4] Therefore I'm careful not to watch anything, whether films or on TV, which could tempt me again. Peter warns us to 'Be alert and of sober mind. Your enemy the devil prowls around like a roaring lion looking for someone to devour.'[5] Temptation is one of the enemy's most common tricks, but we have hope in the promise God gives us through James: 'Resist the devil, and he will flee from you.'[6]

Grace trumps shame

When people used to ask me to tell my story I would leave out porn. Even though I was set free I was still ashamed to talk about what I'd done. This is where my own stupidity had its moment to shine. When God set me free, He also took away my shame. I know that. I felt that. However, it did take me a while to convince myself. I didn't think that I deserved what God had done for me, and I was right. God gives us His incredible, life-saving, transformational grace – which we don't deserve – so we no longer need to feel ashamed or guilty. That's the beauty of the gospel.

I held on to my shame for years, preventing myself from living in the full freedom God had given me.

A few years ago I made a decision to be open and honest – to tell my full story. It's a strange thing in our Church culture that former drug addicts seem more than happy to tell you all about the drugs they used and how messed up they were, and yet porn addicts hide in the pews trying to pretend they never did it. That shouldn't be the case! There are so many people who still struggle with porn and others who still look on them in judgement. We all need educating on this, and it starts with people being open and honest about their experiences. No sin is 'worse' than any other in God's eyes, and we are all equally forgiven, so let's not be afraid to talk about it!

Questions for reflection and discussion

1. When was the first time you were exposed to pornography? How old were you? How did it make you feel?

2. What changes took place in your character and demeanour as a result of your porn use?

3. How can the knowledge that God's grace is free shape your recovery?

2
Why Is Porn a Problem?

Why is porn a problem? It might seem like a strange question to ask. Porn has become a part of our culture, although many of us might not fully realise it or acknowledge it as such. Porn itself is a multi-billion-dollar industry. Statistics from 2010 put that figure at $57 billion.[1] It's not unreasonable to assume that that figure has gone up significantly since then. There are an estimated 4.2 million porn websites online, making up 12 per cent of all websites. There are 68 million daily pornographic search engine requests, making up 25 per cent of all searches. 2.5 billion pornographic emails are sent every day, which is 8 per cent of all emails sent.[2]

That the porn industry operates on such a large scale probably isn't news to you. After all, porn isn't a new phenomenon. When I was at Bible college there was a particular pub where I would go to open mic nights. In the men's toilets above the urinals were framed black-and-white pictures of naked women, which made going to the toilet a somewhat uncomfortable experience for someone training to be a pastor! Old as those pictures were, I'm certain that they didn't represent the beginnings of pornography. Porn has been around for a very long time. The difference now is that it can be found almost anywhere you look.

In my parents' generation, there were two ways to come across porn: in a shop or in the woods. Many a tale is told of young lads sneaking into wooded areas where they found someone's hidden stash of dirty magazines. There's a sense of excitement attached to those stories.

In our current generation, you don't even have to go searching for porn; it finds you. Despite the campaign in 2013 for 'modesty bags' over lads' mags in newsagents, porn is still present at eye level in many shops. Suggestive adverts pop up on people's Facebook pages, purely because they happen to have set their relationship status as 'single'. I was recently followed on Twitter by an account which seemed to be exclusively sharing links to a pornographic Snapchat account, and I've had to block several Instagram porn bots over the last few weeks as well. Porn can be seen in TV adverts, when a woman in a bikini seductively demonstrates the various benefits of some new after-sun lotion which also gives you a tan. That's not to mention the fragrance adverts, which quite often feature nearly naked men and women, with the message seeming to be, 'These people are about to have sex. You should buy our perfume.' You might not think of that as porn, but doesn't that go to show how our perspectives have changed?

I know, you've probably heard all this before, how our society is going down the drain and all we care about is sex and drugs and rock and roll. It's quite a common complaint from the more conservative elements of our culture, and particularly from Christians. I'm not saying that to belittle the Christian voice; after all, I'm a pastor (and before that a Christian, of course). I do feel that at times we don't help ourselves much in the way that we speak about things. We can get preoccupied with speaking out about things we're against and forget to speak about what, or whom, we are for. The Church carries a message of hope in Jesus, but we have become known by some for condemning people's lifestyles. So please don't misunderstand me as I continue in this vein. I am going to talk about porn as a problem, because I believe that it is. What I won't do is condemn or judge those who use it, but my hope is that I can point to a better, healthier way to enjoy your very human, very normal sexual needs.

Dragons, songs and photo hacking

The fact is, our perspectives and our tolerances have changed. It wasn't so long ago that sex scenes weren't a standard part of Hollywood films. At most, you might have a couple beginning to kiss, and then it would be morning. That kind of subtle reference is far less present in films today. It's expected now that there will be at least one sex scene in a film, the graphic nature of which would be determined by the film's rating. Full-frontal nudity is commonplace on television now as well, because of shows like *True Blood* and *Game of Thrones* (to name just two). Those particular shows aren't shy about depicting very graphic sex scenes, and have come under fire for it in the media.

Although full-frontal nudity hasn't made it to daytime television yet, there is still evidence of porn even there. Music videos have become increasingly centred around scantily clad women in recent years. Videos by male artists regularly feature dancers and actresses in sexualised outfits. There appears to be a lot more pressure on young female artists to take their clothes off. I don't want to comment on the quality of the music, but it seems possible that the people in suits over at the record label have discovered that their profits are higher when the singers wear fewer items of clothing. Of course, it's possible that singers decide of their own accord to start portraying themselves in a primarily sexual manner, perhaps to obtain that highly sought-after 'bad girl' image, but I suspect that at some level it comes down to an executive somewhere who understands that there is a lot of money to be made from sexualising pop singers.

Of course, all this has a knock-on effect on the consumers. Cinema-goers now expect to see some depiction of sex on the silver screen. For some, that may be the sole reason for going to see some films. I'm not trying to be cynical here. I can remember clearly when the film *300* came out, one of my friends invited me to go and see it, saying, 'You'll like this film, it has boobs in it.' Television viewers are enticed into watching shows not for the content of their plots (although for many of these shows the plot is actually very compelling), but for the simple fact that at some point in each episode there's a chance they might see boobs. Young girls idolise the singers they see on

TV, and are subconsciously led to believe that the only way boys will be interested in them is if they are prepared to make themselves into sexual objects. Young boys watch these women on TV and start to think that this is normal behaviour for girls, so they expect it from the girls around them.

You may be reading this and thinking that these things are just part of our culture. Hopefully, you're recognising that there's a problem here.

One of the consequences of our tolerances changing as a society is that our boundaries shift as well. As what is 'acceptable' to be shown on TV changes, gradually the same thing happens with people's behaviour in real life. Perhaps the most high-profile example would be the phishing campaign in 2014 which saw nude photos of famous actresses, most notably Jennifer Lawrence, stolen from the actress' personal devices and posted online. Lawrence responded to the hack, saying that her status as a public figure should not give anyone the impression that she had 'asked for this'. She suggested as well that the reason she had originally taken the pictures was that she had been in a long-distance relationship, and that if her boyfriend wasn't looking at her, he'd probably be looking at porn instead.[3]

She went on to call the hack a 'sex crime', including anyone who looked at the pictures among the criminals.

Since many famous actresses regularly appear nude in some form in their films or on TV, the attitude has developed that any images of them belong in the public domain. This is obviously a gross violation of privacy. I believe Jennifer Lawrence was right to classify the hack as a sex crime. After all, if behaviours change, then our definitions ought to change as well. In terms of the violation of privacy, the only thing that makes hacks like this different from the actions of a peeping tom is that the hacker uses a computer instead of a telescope or telephoto lens.

The problem here is one of entitlement. There is no doubt that the actions of these hackers are wrong, but their mindset comes from what they are seeing on their screens. The increasing amount of nudity in TV and films, coupled with ongoing porn use and the anonymity that goes with it, have led a minority of people who populate the less pleasant areas of the internet to believe that they are entitled to view and share any image they come across, regardless of how they come across it. After all, these actresses allow their bodies to be displayed when they are acting, so surely that means the public has the right to any other images there are of them, right? Wrong.

Just for men?

I don't want to portray porn as being a problem for men only. Granted, men are more visually stimulated (generally speaking) than women, so are more likely to struggle with porn. That doesn't mean that women are completely safe from it, though. In fact, as many as 30 to 86 per cent of women are estimated to use porn.[4]

We can't get away from the fact that we're all sexual beings. Each one of us has a libido (sex drive), regardless of gender. For some people this is more active than others. It's important that we don't perpetuate the stereotype that

34

it's only men who enjoy sex, which has been an ingrained part of our society's perception of sex in the past. This perception comes across strongly in the majority of pornography. It is obvious that the primary goal is that the man has a good time. The woman is therefore little more than an object to be used to fulfil the man's sexual desires. This is quite clearly degrading to women, but it also degrades men as well. Porn creates this attitude that women are there to bring pleasure to men, which is horrible, but also that men can or should be OK with that.

There's a mismatch here, which can be seen simply by examining the responses to two people who have sex with several partners. The first, a man, is celebrated by his peers for his apparent aptitude in the bedroom. In some circles he may even appear more attractive to women because of the confidence he gains from so many successful sexual encounters. With each new partner, he feels like more of a success, and comments from those around him only increase his ego.

The second, a woman, is seen by other women as a 'slut'. In the eyes of men, she's 'easy'. These are common phrases, and they are incredibly damaging. The woman who sleeps around is talked about as if she is of no value. To men, she's someone you make lewd jokes about with your mates as you wonder how many people she's slept with. To women, she's like a prostitute, whom they look down on in order to make themselves feel better about their own sex lives.

There seems to be a change in the common dialogue around this issue recently, but not for the better. The recent rise in popularity of feminism has had some very positive effects. However, the approach of modern feminists isn't always all that positive. Feminism, at its heart, is the pursuit of equality between the genders. I'm all for that. In the example of 'stag' and 'slut' labels, feminists appear to be campaigning for women's right to be promiscuous without judgement. That would technically be equality, but wouldn't it be better to instead encourage men to be less driven by sex? Now I agree that 'slut-shaming' people is very damaging, so whatever we do we ought to change that approach, but if our goal is to normalise promiscuity then we've lost the importance of faithfulness, and sex is no more than a hunger to be satisfied on a whim, the way we would eat a cheeseburger.

Men and women respond differently to pornography. Men are visual creatures, and are therefore quite simplistic in the way our libido works. We see an image or video of a naked woman, and we're turned on. Things aren't always so simple for women.

Of course, some women are similarly visually stimulated. There has been a rise in the last few years in what is known as 'mommy porn' – porn made by and for women.[5] Mommy porn videos tend to have a romantic focus, with more dialogue and backstory before the hardcore content begins. Included within this category of mommy porn is literary porn, or 'erotica'. Erotica invites the reader to engage their imagination, through very descriptive stories of sexual encounters. The heroine of the story may be a generic kind of character, and deliberately so, to make it easy for a wide variety of readers to put themselves in her place.

Erotica appears harmless; many erotica books might not even be viewed as porn, but that is what they are. Some of these may not even be officially classed as erotica; they are simply romantic novels, which have increasingly come to include more graphic sexual scenes within their stories.

This kind of fiction has become mainstream in the past few years. When E L James published her book *Fifty Shades of Grey*, at first people were a little shocked to hear what it was about. A story about a young woman becoming infatuated with a rich, older man, who leads her into a new kind of sexual relationship centred around her relinquishing control of her body to him wasn't something 'normal' people were accustomed to reading.

As with all things that shock, word spread and, before long, people were buying the book out of curiosity, because it couldn't possibly be as graphic as they say, could it? It might look slightly different, but the pattern is the same as when a man glimpses a pornographic image, and decides to take what he thinks will be a harmless second look. Now, *Fifty Shades of Grey* is a worldwide bestseller and a blockbuster film.

Books like *Fifty Shades of Grey* are not classed as pornography, and therefore are considered acceptable even within some Christian circles. This is a perception that needs to change. We find it perfectly normal to see conventional pornography as a sinful activity, but either through lack of awareness or a voluntary ignorance of its effects, we've developed a blind spot where the sexualised written word is concerned. It seems that this can be more of a problem for women than it is for men. As Debra Fileta suggests, this is a mismatch in values, in that some women who eagerly watch these kinds of films or read these kinds of books would be offended by their spouses watching porn.[6]

Of course, sex had been a part of written fiction for a long time before *Fifty Shades* came out. Erotica may not have been out in the open the way it is now, but it wouldn't be unusual to find graphic sex scenes in mainstream romantic novels as well.

I myself have several times had to reconsider the kind of novels I am reading because of the sexual content. This is particularly hard when it's a very good story! I'm the kind of person who has to finish something once I've started it – I need to know how it ends. However, there has been more than one series of books which I have chosen to stop reading, never to find out the ending, because I found the graphic descriptions of sexual encounters caused me to visualise things I didn't want to be visualising.

It may be useful for you to apply to the written word the same filters you would use with TV or film. Is it helpful for you to be reading this kind of material? Are you allowing temptation to gain a foothold in your life through what you're reading?

Porn can become a debilitating problem if it is given space to do so. It might start off small and seemingly innocent, but curiosity very quickly becomes dependence. Let's consider how this can begin.

The first time

Porn is widely regarded as an adult pastime. Censors refer to it as 'adult content'. However, statistics show that the average age of first exposure is eleven, with the highest consumption of online pornography being from those aged twelve to seventeen.[7] This first exposure typically happens in one of two ways.

1. **Discovery.** The child accidentally stumbles upon a box hidden away somewhere. This probably happens when they're playing hide-and-seek, or just looking for a lost toy. When they open the box, they discover that its contents are far more interesting than whatever it was they were looking for. There are images there that they'd never even thought about before. For reasons they can't explain, the images excite them. It's a new experience, both pleasant and confusing.

   Once they've overcome the initial shock of discovery, they may begin to wonder why this box was hidden away. Obviously they weren't supposed to find it. Maybe Mummy doesn't even know about it. If that's the case, it must be very valuable. Experts equate this experience to finding buried treasure. The very fact that it was hidden makes it more exciting. The child then begins to keep it secret. If they're particularly bold they'll take something from the box to hide themselves, and the circle of secretive behaviour continues.

2. **Older, bolder friends.** Some children have a friend or relative who is just a little bit older than them, whom they look up to. Often that friend or relative enjoys the feeling of being a role model. If the older friend or relative goes through the process above, they may at some point decide to share their discovery with their younger friend or relative. With great excitement, they

lead the other child to the place where they've hidden the little bit they took from Dad's box. Holding it behind their back, they build up the tension and expectation in the other child before revealing their secret. The excitement they experienced upon finding the porn stash is then passed on to the younger child. You may recall from my story the friend who brought a pornographic playing card into school, aged eight, or the friend who got bored of wrestling games and directed us to online porn. It's the same principle.

These kinds of experiences are more common than you'd think. It's quite probable that before sex education has been taught in school, many of the children will have seen a pornographic image of some description already. It might be that the first experience was a one-off, or even was so much of a shock that the child never seeks it out again. However, for some it will have piqued their interest just enough that they keep returning to the stash, or search further afield for more images. Sooner or later, what they've already found won't be enough.

Curiosity killed the intimacy

Sexual desire is something that we all experience. It's a normal part of life, of which we become aware at some point during our early teenage years. During those years, we try our best to come to terms with this new phenomenon, which seems to have turned girls from horrible creatures with plastic ponies that we wouldn't go near, to the most desirable creatures on planet Earth, whose attentions we desire more than scoring the winning goal in a football match or getting good GCSE results.[8]

During our teenage years, there are many voices around us trying to tell us how to interpret our sexual desires. The media (and consequently, our friends as well) tell us that the best way to figure it out is to find someone to have sex with us. Our teachers awkwardly deliver a sex education curriculum which is sadly based on the assumption that most young people will sleep around by default. Therefore, its content is mostly geared towards how to avoid sexually transmitted infections and unwanted pregnancy. I get that this is important, but the education system completely ignores the central issue of our sexual urges – intimacy.

Youth leaders in churches I'm aware of are doing a great job of trying to present a biblical perspective on sexual relationships, but it's not an easy subject to deal with. While I do believe that sex is something God created to be enjoyed exclusively in the context of marriage, that simple truth on its own is far from helpful for hormonal teenagers who are desperately trying to figure out who they are and how to behave around the opposite sex. In the midst of all these conflicting voices vying for young people's attention is the subversive voice of porn. This is one key reason why I believe that porn is a dangerous problem.

We are created as sexual beings. I believe that there are two goals for our God-given sexual desire: intimacy and pregnancy. Porn achieves neither of these things. It is a pale imitation of the intimacy experienced between a married couple having sex. It's just sex.

Just sex.

The problem here is that we've been sold a false purpose for sexual desire. Porn tells us that the reason you have urges is so that you can experience pleasure. Obviously there is some truth to that. Sex is a very pleasurable experience, and I believe that God intended it to be so. However, pleasure is not the sole purpose of sex. Sex for pleasure alone is selfish. If that was the only purpose for our sexual desires, then porn would be an adequate expression of them. Watching people have sex is a pleasurable experience, which leads the viewer into other pleasurable experiences as they explore their own body.

I think that most people who have used pornography will on some level recognise that it didn't fully satisfy them. When the experience was over, they were left feeling frustrated and disappointed. That's because sex isn't just about pleasure. People turn to porn out of a desire to feel some kind of connection to someone else. Porn pretends to offer that, but instead gives you a vicarious experience through watching actors having 'just sex'. As pleasurable as that experience is, it only lasts a moment, and it can never give you the object of your sexual desire – intimacy. The disappointment that arises from that can lead people into more interactive forms of pornography such as cybersex and prostitution.

Porn is a problem because it pretends to be an easy alternative to appropriate sexual relationships. In the short term, it fulfils a sexual need, but in the long term it damages self-esteem and destroys the intimacy of existing and even future relationships. Watching porn is an addictive activity. Just like any other addiction, it is very difficult to break the habit. Throughout this book, my aim is to show that the habit can be broken, and that it is possible to discover a healthy concept of sexuality afterwards.

Questions for reflection and discussion

1. How do you see sex portrayed in the media? If you're honest with yourself, how has that shaped your own view of sex?

2. How did your first contact with porn come about? What did you feel in that moment?

3. Do you agree that porn in itself does not satisfy? Why would you say that is?

3
Discovering Intimacy

Intimacy is not a word that you'd be likely to find in regular use today in ordinary conversation. I can't think of a time when I've seen it appear in any of the many WhatsApp groups I'm in. The thought of saying to a group of friends, 'I really just want to experience intimacy,' is more than a little bit odd. And yet, intimacy is something we all crave on some level.

It's possible that we don't use the word so often in everyday conversation because our desire for intimacy is quite a personal thing. Therefore, it's not something most of us would feel comfortable to express to anyone except our very closest friends. Some people may be prepared to talk about sex, but less so about intimacy. Why is that?

I think it's because there's more to intimacy than sexual contact with another person. I do believe that sex is the most intimate thing two people can physically do together. The joining together of two bodies is incredibly intimate, and yet it is possible to have lots of sex but lack intimacy.

To understand why, we need to first grasp the purpose for which intimacy was created.

It is not good

Let's take a look at the very beginning – the book of Genesis. Genesis tells us that God created the heavens and the earth. He created oceans and skies, plants and animals, and finally He created man. At each stage, God declared His work to be 'good', with the exception of the man, who God called 'very good'. The man, called Adam, was placed in a beautiful garden and given the job of looking after it. Once this is established, we see a very interesting insight into the mind of God.

> Then the LORD God said, 'It is not good for the man
> to be alone. I will make a helper who is just right for
> him.'[1]

Notice the language there. Up until this point, everything was 'good' in the eyes of God. The very first thing God ever declared to be 'not good' was the man's loneliness. The commentator Kenneth Mathews gives a very insightful thought on this when he says:

> God has created human life to have fellowship with
> him but also to be a social entity, building
> relationships with other human beings.[2]

In Mathews' comment, we see two purposes in the creation of man: fellowship with God and relationship with other human beings. Right from the very beginning,

God was all about relationship. That word 'fellowship' refers to a deep and personal relationship, like that of close friends or family. God wants us to know Him intimately.

On some level, we all feel a need to relate to other people. You may have heard the saying, 'No man is an island.' [3] While we all have different capacities for relationships – some people have many people they would call close friends, others have few – one thing we all have in common is a need for them. Figures from January 2017 show that 2.789 billion people actively use social media around the world (that's up 21 per cent from January 2016).[4] The rise of social media reveals to us how central relationships are to life as a human being. However, connecting with people on social media doesn't necessarily produce intimate friendships.

I have 709 friends on Facebook. That's probably a relatively small number, compared to others, but it's still way more people than I can possibly claim to know on a personal level. Most of them are people I've met IRL (in real life), which is perhaps why my total may be smaller than some other users', but few of them are people I would count as close friends. I do spend quite a bit of my time on social media, but I've never felt that they could or should become the primary way I interact with my close friends and family. Perhaps you feel the same way too. So what is it that's missing from social media?

The simple answer: intimacy. Sure, it's possible to develop some level of relational intimacy using a messaging service and video chat, but usually there comes a point when a face-to-face meeting takes place. That's because there's no substitute for being physically present with someone if you want to really get to know them. As Craig Groeschel puts it:

> We have lots of online interactivity, but that doesn't mean we have any personal intimacy.[5]

Defining intimacy

Our goal here is to discover a better kind of intimacy, but it seems that, before we can do that, we need to have a clearer idea of what intimacy means. Derek Kidner writes, commenting on the Genesis passage:

> [Man] will not live until he loves, giving himself away to another on his own level.[6]

Kidner's comment gives us a good and useable definition of intimacy: giving oneself away to another on his (or her) own level. This can apply across the whole spectrum of relationships, from platonic friendships, marriage, all the way to the most intimate and important relationship: your relationship with God. Of course, the way it applies across that spectrum will look different according to the context of each relationship. Your relationship to someone you're friendly with at work or school should not be intimate in the same way as your relationship to a spouse; that would be weird and inappropriate.

Intimacy in a platonic friendship might entail choosing to share personal information with them. I'm not talking about your contact details here, although that is a start! I'm talking about choosing to trust your friend with things you wouldn't tell someone you don't know. This kind of friendship is the kind where you can talk about yourself openly, knowing that your friend will respect you and not share that information with anyone else. As part of that trust, you also do the same for your friend. You probably have at least one friend like this. Have you ever thought of that friendship as being intimate?

A romantic relationship greatly extends this emotional intimacy, and adds in a new level of physical intimacy. This is appropriately expressed in different ways, depending on the level of romantic relationship. Hand-holding, cuddling, gazing longingly into one another's eyes (there's no touch involved in that one, but it still counts as physical intimacy) and similar could be considered comparatively 'safe' ways of expressing physical intimacy in a dating relationship. Depending on your personal conviction, kissing can be included in that list. I say that because there are people who, for perfectly legitimate reasons, choose not to kiss at all before marriage. Once the relationship becomes a marriage, many more ways to express physical intimacy become available.

Genesis gives us the first instance of both sexual intercourse and marriage. It is no accident that the two occur in the same passage.

> That is why a man leaves his father and mother and
> is united to his wife, and they become one flesh.[7]

This notion of 'one flesh' is the reason why sexual intimacy is intended for a marriage relationship. There is

49

more involved in sexual intimacy than simply the biological act of having sex. In this one verse we see two key elements that make up this relationship.

1. **Leaving.** It's not actually a requirement for a person to move out of their parents' house in order to get married (although it does help if you can!). This 'leaving' signifies a change in life situation. A person doesn't enter into marriage expecting nothing to change in their life. Before there is a sexual element to the relationship, there is first a commitment made between the two partners.

2. **Uniting.** Marriage is both a legal contract and a spiritual covenant. In it, the couple swear an oath to be joined together for the rest of their lives. Marriage unites every element of life: finances, possessions, location, legal obligations and sexual intimacy. Out of this uniting, the husband and wife become 'one flesh'. As Dietrich Bonhoeffer puts it:

> It is best to describe this unity by saying that he now belongs to her because she belongs to him. They are no longer one without the other; they are one and yet two.[8]

Sexual intimacy is intended for marriage because it is the expression of a far deeper commitment – that of becoming 'one' with another person. This is not something that can be done on a whim, or based simply on physical desire for a person. That is why, in the introduction to a wedding ceremony, the minister says these words:

In marriage, husband and wife belong to one another and begin a new life within the community. It is a way of life that all should honour and must not be undertaken carelessly, lightly or selfishly, but reverently and responsibly and after serious thought.[9]

God created sexual intimacy to be enjoyed by a man and a woman who have made this deepest of commitments to one another. Within that context, sexual intimacy finds its fullest expression, because a couple who have committed so deeply to one another have achieved intimacy on more than just a physical level. It's a myth that marriage equals boring sex; quite the opposite![10] William Struthers sums it up excellently:

The need for intimacy requires that we understand who we are and share that with those we long to be known by. As we become more intimate, the other speaks into us things about ourselves that we could not possibly know from the inside. We allow the one we are intimate with to discover us in ways we could not do on our own, and we do so with them. It is a process that develops and deepens over time. We know ourselves more fully because we are known more fully.[11]

Intimacy with God

Intimacy with other human beings is a vital part of life for most of us. Few would deny that, although the desire for that intimacy is expressed differently by different people.

What is perhaps less widely accepted, and yet far more important, is our need for intimacy with God. Psychologist Gerald May, reflecting upon his years of practising therapy, writes:

> After twenty years of listening to the yearnings of people's hearts, I am convinced that human beings have an inborn desire for God. Whether we are consciously religious or not, this desire is our deepest longing and most precious treasure.[12]

God is our Creator. He formed each of us in our mothers' wombs,[13] He has loved us with an everlasting love,[14] and He laid down His life for us.[15] That same God invites each of us to have a close and personal relationship with Him. There is one thing that gets in the way of us enjoying this relationship; the Bible calls it sin. The good news is that Jesus' death on the cross and resurrection has broken down that barrier and made a way for us to come to God.[16]

> Christianity is not about our disciplined pursuit of God, but about God's relentless pursuit of us – to the point of dying on a cross for us that we might become his friends.[17]

Even though Jesus has made a way for us to come to God, we can still let our sin cause a barrier for us. When I was using porn, I wasn't able to experience intimacy with God. This was partly because of the shame I felt over what I was doing, and partly because I was still more interested in the pleasure (momentary though it was) that porn offered than I was in connecting with God. Ken Shigematsu says:

If our connection with God has been severed or compromised, we will be more likely to look for intimacy in unhealthy ways, seeking some kind of substitute for the eternal embrace each of us longs for.[18]

This is exactly what we are doing when we try to fill our lives with porn. There is a need, deep within each of us, to be loved. For many, this seems to extend only as far as a need to be loved by other people, but in reality it goes further: we all have a deep need to be loved by God.

Intimacy with God is knowing Him and being known by Him. It's about prayer – real prayer, which is not simply reeling off requests to God like our Christmas wish list. The kind of prayer that brings intimacy with God is a conversation – two-sided. We talk to God, but we also listen to Him and expect Him to speak to us. Oswald Chambers says:

Do not have as your motive the desire to be known as a praying person. Get an inner chamber in which to pray where no one knows you are praying, shut the door, and talk to God in secret. Have no other motive than to know your Father in heaven.[19]

Or perhaps Jesus said it better:

When you pray, go into your room, close the door and pray to your Father, who is unseen. Then your

Father, who sees what is done in secret, will reward you.[20]

What is that reward which Jesus mentions? 'God himself is the reward of Christians.' [21] Our reward for spending time in the private place of prayer is intimacy with God our heavenly Father.

During the years after Jesus set me free from porn, I often wrongly felt unable to come to God in the secret place, because of the shame I still felt over what I'd done. Perhaps the most important lesson I've learned in the years since is that my past shame does not disqualify me from coming to God – in fact, He wants me to, in spite of it! It is only by coming into the presence of our heavenly Father and spending time there that we can come to a place of fully accepting what Jesus has done for us in removing our sin.

There is a better kind of intimacy than the false one offered by porn. It is open to all, regardless of anything we've done in the past. Nobody is disqualified from intimacy with God. But we will have to stop some things in order to access it, because continuing sinful activity will have an effect on our intimacy with Him.

What if you chose to spend time in the secret place with God, and discovered everything you've ever been looking for is freely available to you there?

Questions for reflection and discussion

1. What does the word 'intimacy' mean to you?

2. Who are the people in your life with whom you would say you have an intimate relationship? What kind of intimacy is represented by each of these relationships?

3. Do you experience intimacy with God? If not, what can you do to begin to experience this?

4
Porn and Technology

Adolescence is a period when we strive to find ourselves, outside the immediate influence of our parents. It's a time when we go through myriad physical and emotional changes, which leave us wondering who we really are. For many people, adolescence is a tumultuous time. As a result, young people are particularly susceptible to the allures of pornography. For me, it was very much a case of curiosity that led me to explore porn. I'd caught a glimpse of what sex looked like, and I wanted to see more.

As we have discovered, porn is far easier to access now than it ever has been. This is not only an issue for young people, but they are more susceptible as the first generation to grow up with open access to the internet. In this chapter I will discuss issues relating to technology and young people, including advice for parents on how to protect children and young people from accessing inappropriate material. Despite this focus on young people, the principles of what I'll discuss to do with technology apply to anyone who regularly uses such devices.

Wi-Fi, Wi-Fi, Wi-Fi, Delilah?

The internet has vastly changed the landscape of our society. Since its inception, the internet has permeated our very lives, to the point that many of us can't function without it. I can recall times in recent years when our office Wi-Fi has been frustratingly intermittent. As a result, our staff team have discovered just now little we can actually get done without the internet!

I'm not about to say that the internet is a bad thing. I happen to like the internet. I use it every day, in a variety of formats. As I write this, my smartphone is sitting next to me, connected to the internet, as is my tablet. Should I so desire, I could turn on my games console and use it to watch the video-streaming service of my choice on my TV – or to play a game, for that matter. I could even browse the internet on my computer – the very same computer with which I am writing this book! I know, you're shocked. What I'm saying is, the internet can be a good thing.

However, it can also a very bad thing. All those devices that I mentioned, all those means that we have to access the internet wherever we are, whenever we want – great as that facility is – are a part of the problem. In the year 2000, Henry Rogers wrote a book called *The Silent War*.[1] In it, he predicted that as technology advanced, the problem of pornography would worsen exponentially. Since the year 2000, technology has indeed advanced, providing us with high-speed fibre-optic broadband, which can be accessed wirelessly by a plethora of devices. We have also been blessed with that ever-faithful companion – the smartphone. There's a very telling meme I've seen a few times online, which shows the progression of mobile phones. It starts with massive 'bricks', with each model getting smaller, but then there's a change where the picture notes the point at which we discovered we could use our phones to watch porn. After that point, screens seem to get bigger and bigger. I'd say that Henry Rogers has been proved right.

When I was a teenager, we had one computer in our house – one point of access to the internet – with a dial-up connection that provided an almighty cacophony when you connected to it. Personally, as much as I love the constant availability of fibre-optic broadband, I do miss singing along to our dial-up modem. Dial-up also required you to choose between using the internet and using the telephone. How things have changed! It is quite normal today for the majority of people to have access to multiple internet-capable devices. I'm sure that as you're reading this you're probably no more than one metre away from at least one such device. If you've been particularly struck by something you've read so far, you might have picked up your phone and tweeted it. It's OK, that's allowed.

Where porn fits in

Let's add porn into the mix, then. Here are some statistics for you:

- Approximately 25 per cent of all web searches are for pornography.

- It is estimated that 2.5 billion emails per day contain pornography; this represents 8 per cent of daily emails sent.

- 10 per cent of all adult internet users believe they are porn addicts.

- The average age of first exposure to pornography is eleven.

- 70 per cent of teenagers admit to having seen pornographic images online.[2]

These are just the reported figures. I suspect that the real figures would make those numbers look small.

The internet provides absolute anonymity to those searching for porn. We saw in Chapter 2 how not so long ago you would have to sneak into the woods, or go to a shop to access porn. If you were in the latter category, you would have to come into contact with an actual person in order to buy the magazine or video. There was a risk that you might run into someone you knew, and then they would know that you bought porn. You may also have had to go to an adult book shop, with the added risk of simply being seen on the premises by someone you knew. There's no mistaking why you'd be in there! With the internet, you can cut out that risk.

Perhaps a more practical by-product of that is that you now have to expend little to no effort to obtain pornography. There's no need to walk to the newsagents, or skulk around outside the adult shop to make sure nobody sees you go in or come out. You can just click your mouse or tap your screen, type some things into your favourite search engine, and you're away. That goes for young people too. There's no shop assistant to tell them that they're younger than eighteen, so can't purchase a copy of a dirty magazine. The only barrier now is a button to press which 'confirms' that the user is over eighteen, and even that only appears on genuine porn sites. Simply flicking over to the 'Discover' tab on Instagram can lead to accessing sexualised images within seconds, with no barriers at all. It is easier than ever to access porn.

If you're a parent, this might not be brand-new information to you, but perhaps you've been wondering what you could possibly do about it. Unfortunately, there are limits to what you can do to protect your children from coming into contact with porn, particularly when they're out of the house and subject to external influences of which you may not be aware. Even so, don't lose hope! There are some things you can do which will go some way to keeping your children safe from porn.

The simplest action you can take is to limit their internet use to one computer or tablet, and only when others are in the room. Don't allow them to take their devices to bed with them. This might seem a bit controlling, and your children might well see it that way. After all, 91 per cent of young people say they take their phone or tablet to bed with them.[3] If you're also a regular user of a smartphone or tablet, you might find it helpful to adjust your own habits as well, so that this is something you do as a family. That way, it doesn't have to be obviously about protecting your children from porn; it can become about creating time as a family to be together regularly without the distraction of technology.

It can be possible to oversee the content your children are accessing in a non-invasive way. Software is available in a variety of formats, which filters the content you access, and either blocks out porn or flags it and sends a report to an accountability partner – some software requires the user to assign accountability partners, who receive a weekly email from the software detailing the kind of things the user has accessed online during that time. If no questionable content has been accessed, the email will simply say so, but if the user has been looking at porn the accountability partner will receive a table containing all the websites viewed, how many times they were viewed, what time they were viewed at and the reasons why they have been flagged as questionable.

While these types of software are great, they're most helpful for those who are already involved in porn use and are trying to stop. They can also be turned off by the user, if they were the one to register it, so it is recommended that one of the accountability partners sets it up, using a password that only they know. A couple of well-known examples of these kinds of software are X3Watch and Covenant Eyes.

These days it's almost a necessity of modern life to own a smartphone. Recent statistics estimate that as many as 74 per cent of teenagers owns one.[4] These devices are great, but it's very easy to access porn on them. If you're looking to buy one for your child, my recommendation is that you put them on a plan without cellular data. In other words, get them a plan which doesn't allow their phone to access the internet except for using Wi-Fi. It's not foolproof, but it'll at least mean that your child is less at risk of viewing porn outside your home, where you can monitor them. Unfortunately, there is very little you can do about the availability of free-to-access Wi-Fi networks in public. That being the case, it's worth installing some form of screening app or software on their phone as well.

I don't want to sound like a broken record (the irony of using that metaphor when writing about modern technology is not lost on me), but it's so important that we get to grips with shielding ourselves and our young people from pornographic content.

When technology goes wrong

There have been quite a few stories in the news over the last few years of sexual abuse and manipulation occurring in schools. The common theme in these stories is technology. *The Telegraph* ran a story in the wake of the death of a thirteen-year-old girl who had reportedly been pressurised into performing a sexual act on a boy at her school, which he had filmed on his mobile phone and sent to his friends. She threatened to jump out of a fourth-floor window unless he deleted the footage, and fell to her death in the process. This is one incident illustrating a new problem among schoolchildren; young people now have the means to film pornographic material for themselves using their smartphones, and distribute this footage to their friends without the consent of those featured.[5] The article quotes psychologist Steve Biddulph:

> Never before has girlhood been under such a sustained assault – from ads, alcohol marketing,

girls' magazines, sexually explicit TV programmes and the hard pornography that is regularly accessed in so many teenagers' bedrooms.

We need to be more vigilant than ever if we are to protect our children and young people from exposure to inappropriate content online. It may feel like there is little that can be done by parents, since the children spend so much time out of the house either at school or with their friends. It is true that there is a limit to what parents can do, but being able to put into place measures to protect the home from adult content is a significant step in the right direction. The suggestions I've made in this chapter are by no means an exhaustive list. I encourage you to be proactive and search online for other means to protect your children. It may not be possible to completely screen children from inappropriate content, but it is entirely possible to place limits on it, and that is a very good place to start.

Questions for reflection and discussion

1. How many devices do you have which are able to access porn? What are you doing to protect yourself and your family?

2. Are there changes you need to make to the way and amount you use technology, to prevent temptation?

3. Are you prepared to set up some accountability software on your devices to help guard you from temptation?

5
Porn and Education

Earlier in the book I told the story of how I was first shown pornographic images by a friend in the playground, in the form of a playing card. Given that the majority of teenagers own smartphones, today's equivalent of my friend's dirty playing card is a simple Google Image search. I admit that I've found myself shocked by the accounts of pornographic material being viewed, shared or even made by children in schools as I've carried out research for this book.

Porn has become a problem for young people in a way it never has been before. As a result, the government has been working on rewriting the curriculum on sex education, which is a positive step. However, more needs to be done to equip and encourage parents so that they can more effectively educate their children about proper conduct with the opposite sex.

Since very few girls would be willing to tell a teacher that a boy had sexual footage of her on his phone, it's difficult for schools to combat this problem properly. That's not to say that there's nothing to be done, though, and Ofsted have made it known that they want to see changes in the way schools handle the issue of sex and relationships with pupils. In 2013, Ofsted produced a report into schools' provision of Personal, Social, Health and Economic education (PSHE), and found that in one-third of schools the curriculum on sex and relationships needed to be improved. The report states:

> In secondary schools it [the poor quality of teaching] was because too much emphasis was placed on 'the mechanics' of reproduction and too little on relationships, sexuality, the influence of pornography on students' understanding of healthy sexual relationships, dealing with emotions and staying safe.[1]

My own observation of sex education in school was very similar to the findings of the Ofsted report. My parents had been quite willing to talk to me about sex, so by the time it was covered in school I already knew that babies aren't brought by storks, that sex has nothing to do with birds and bees, and that there was much more involved than simply a mummy and a daddy loving each other very much and having a 'special cuddle'. I was also brought up to believe that sex was something that you only do with your wife or husband.

In school, it was simply a biology lesson. 'This bit goes in here, but make sure you use protection or you'll get a disease or a baby.' I'm not saying that this doesn't need to be taught, but there's more going on in the mind of a teenager than the simple mechanics of it all. Granted, most teenagers are curious about that, but on a deeper level there's a lot of emotional stuff that needs to be addressed.

At that time, you're going through puberty. Your body is changing, and the teachers will tell you about that, but what about how you feel about it? Maybe your facial hair doesn't come in as thick as the other boys', or your breasts take a lot longer to appear than the other girls'. There's insecurity and uncertainty there – a fight to figure out your identity – and all you're told is a list of changes that you're supposed to go through, and how to avoid getting an STD. I can still remember the inner turmoil of those years, watching all the other kids around me develop while I seemed (to myself at least) to be going much slower.

I'm not trying to evoke sympathy here. It's not like I was years behind my peers and bullied as a result. I'm aware that you may be reading this book now and that was your experience through puberty. Whether you had an easy ride through that season or not, have a think back to the kind of teaching you were given on sex when you were at school. In my school, the attitude was that we would all be having sex as soon as we could. In fact, I remember a teacher saying, 'We'll be holding more sex education classes next year. Most of you will be doing it by then.' There was no hint that perhaps that wasn't the best approach to sex and relationships.

The good news is that since 2013, the government has been making progress on this issue. While there is still a long way to go, the findings of the 2013 report are beginning to be implemented. So far, the only compulsory element of sex and relationship education (SRE) is the scientific side – including how to avoid sexually transmitted infections. However, the government is changing the focus of the curriculum by renaming it 'Relationship and Sex Education'. Although this is just a simple switching of word order, it communicates the greater value being placed upon teaching young people about healthy relationships as a part of their sexual education.[2]

I'm encouraged by this change, because it signals the beginning of a more healthy approach to teaching about sex and relationships. I firmly believe that the only healthy context for a sexual relationship is marriage. It's so important that we don't shy away from that issue just because it's not the generally accepted way to do things. Having said that, I want to be very clear that I do not believe that marriage is a solution to problems with porn. If these issues aren't addressed before marriage, they will become problems within the marriage. If you're already married and struggling with porn, I urge you to be honest with your spouse, hard as that is, while seeking help.

It's not normal

I used to help out with the Friday night youth work at our church, which was run by my wife, Annie. Our team occasionally had the opportunity for conversations with the young people, most of whom weren't Christians, about relationships. When I had those conversations, many of the young people were surprised that I was married. I think that they were mostly surprised because we both seemed so young to them. We were in our early to mid-twenties when we got married, which is not unusual, especially in

Christian circles, but wasn't normal to the young people in our youth club. They would ask me all sorts of questions, which gave me the opportunity to talk to them about what it means to be committed to – and only sleeping with – one person for life. That concept was alien to some of them!

Some of the young people we were meeting had faced pregnancy scares, had their hearts broken by others who had slept with them and then slept with their friend, or simply regretted going as far as they did with someone. None of this should be surprising, since nobody seemed to be teaching them about appropriate sexual relationships. No wonder porn is an issue as well!

The Ofsted report I mentioned earlier cited inadequate training as one of the reasons why sex education was not good enough in schools. If our children and young people are to grow up with a healthy perspective on sex, their teachers and their parents need to be equipped to provide that education.

I'm very thankful that my parents felt able to talk to me about sex from a young age. They always presented things in a way that was appropriate to my age, which meant that when it came to my first sex education classes in school, I wasn't blindsided and neither was I over-informed. There were things which my parents didn't teach me; they didn't go into detail about how to actually have sex – that would have been very awkward (not to mention inappropriate)! What they did was demonstrate that talking about sex doesn't have to be uncomfortable. It still might not be the favourite conversation topic over a family dinner, but we need to get past our fear of awkwardness in order to prepare children and young people for what they will learn in school.

If you are a parent and you're worried about what is being taught to your children in sex education, I encourage you to make enquiries with their school. Find out what is on the curriculum, and if it concerns you then raise those concerns with the school. It may also be helpful to write to your MP, since some of the issues with the curriculum will need to be handled at a governmental level.

Pornography is no longer a minority problem that can be ignored. Those of us who are in a position to influence young people around us – parents, teachers, youth leaders, pastors, whatever your role is in interacting with young people – have an incredibly important role to play in safeguarding this generation against the very real threat that porn is to their sexual identities.

Tell them why

I was recently invited by a neighbouring church to speak at their evening service. The service was run by their youth pastor, whose aim was to create an environment geared towards young people/young adults while also including the older generations in the church.

The church had been doing a series during those evening services about relationships, and the topic I was given on which to speak was 'What Sex Really Isn't'. I couldn't resist poking fun at the title slightly, because there are a lot of things sex really isn't – for instance, it isn't a public activity!

I began by sharing some of the really bad teaching I'd heard about sex when I was a teenager myself. Phrases like 'Don't touch what you don't have' or 'Keep your feet on the ground' were often the motto of so-called Abstinence Teaching. There are several problems with this kind of slogan, not the least of which is that there is a great deal that a couple of teenagers can do together which would fall within the letter of these laws if not the heart behind them. After all, we all have bums and nipples!

As I've reflected on what I was taught about sex when I was growing up, I've come to realise the core issue which was not addressed: the why of it all. Much like the PSHE lessons which Ofsted rightly identified as 'not yet good enough', the teaching of church youth groups has sometimes failed to instil in young people the reason why such teaching is presented to them. If a reason is given, it may amount simply to 'because the Bible says so'. While I would never want to cast aspersions on the authority of the Bible, I don't believe that it should ever be used as a kind of trump card with no explanation as to why. This is particularly important when speaking to young people, because many of them will naturally react negatively if they are told to believe or do something without any reason being given as to why.

I'm not for a second denying that the Bible does indeed teach abstinence outside marriage. [3] However, for a teenager who struggles daily with raging hormones and pressure from those around them to be sexually active, there has to be more to abstinence teaching; we have to explain why.

If we want our young people to be safe from pornography and from unhealthy sexual relationships, we need to capture their hearts with something more valuable than those things. One of the biggest lies our young people are being told is that sex is the pinnacle of human experience. Those who have had it (or claim to have had it) are held up to be somehow better than those who have not. To be known to be a virgin is humiliating. This is why some young people will loudly brag to their friends about their sexual encounters, even if such encounters are purely fictional. Sex is the most important experience one can have, in the eyes of many young people.

I'm going to be quite controversial here. Take a moment to prepare yourself. Are you ready? Here we go.

Sex isn't *that* good.

While you're picking your jaw up from the floor, let me qualify that statement. I don't want you to read this and panic about the state of my marriage. Sex is good, but it isn't *that* good.

If we look to sex to fulfil us as human beings, we'll be sorely disappointed. God created sex to be a pleasurable experience, but it was never intended to bring fulfilment to our lives in any meaningful way. Teenagers are led to believe that having sex is an essential rite of passage into adulthood, after which they can be considered to have 'lived'. This is a deeply damaging deceit, not the least because the first time is rarely an earth-shatteringly amazing experience for either partner. Sex has been built up to be an essential part of life. It's no wonder so many people use sex to try to fix their self-esteem issues, but it's also no surprise that it fails every time. If you're trying to use sex to find fulfilment in life, it's not going to work. Sex isn't *that* good. Dallas Willard illustrates it this way:

> If the places in our blood cells designed to carry oxygen are occupied by carbon monoxide, we die for lack of oxygen. If the places in our souls that are to be indwelt by God and his service are occupied by food, sex and society, we die or languish for lack of God and right relation to his creatures. A proper abstinence actually breaks the hold of improper engagements so that the soul can be properly engaged in and by God.[4]

How, then, do we combat this prevailing attitude among our young people? What could possibly replace sex in the minds of teenagers as the single greatest thing they could seek? The answer to those questions is the same as the answer to any Sunday school question: Jesus. We need something more than just the dry old abstinence teaching – which at best fills young people with guilt whenever they are confronted by their sexual desires, and at worst drives them to pursue sex out of rebellion; we need the message of the gospel. In our search for something exciting to present to young people which will capture their hearts, we need look no further than Jesus.

True disciples of Jesus seek with every breath they take to emulate Him and become more like Him. They do this not out of obligation or subscription to a set of rules but out of love for the God who first loved them. We need to introduce our young people to Jesus, who came to bring them life in all its abundance.[5] The claim of society is that sex will fulfil their desire for belonging and purpose, but the only way those desires can be fulfilled is through relationship with Jesus. Pursuit of pleasure and popularity does not result in abundant life; following Jesus does.

If you're a young person reading this and you don't know Jesus, why don't you flick to the back and find the Resources section? Get your smartphone out and check out some of the websites listed there, which will tell you about Jesus. Read about His life, watch videos explaining who He is and what He has to say to you. Discover for yourself this Jesus who loves you and died for you, so that you could live the greatest life possible.

If you're a youth leader or parent, make it your goal in any teaching on sex and relationships to introduce your young people to Jesus first and foremost. In any conversation you have about sex, show them that it all comes back to Jesus. If you can inspire them by your example and your words to follow Jesus and know Him for themselves, they will be able and open to discover the reason why the Bible tells them to keep themselves pure.

There is no quick fix for this; I wish there were. I don't believe that anyone has come up with a formula for keeping young people away from porn and unhealthy sexual relationships. Our starting point has to be the why of it all. I remained a virgin until I got married, largely because I felt guilty about the prospect of premarital sex. There was a part of me which was worried that I would continue to feel that sex was a thing to feel guilty for, even once I was married. I'm thankful that I did not. It wasn't until I began to reflect upon the teaching I'd heard on sex as a teenager that I realised the simple truth that if I'd met Jesus personally and decided to follow Him sooner than I did I might have understood more readily and obeyed out of love, not out of guilt.

Questions for reflection and discussion

1. What was your sex education like in school? What effect, if any, did it have on your perceptions of sex and relationships?

2. What was the general perception of sex like in your friendship group? What effect did that have on you?

3. Have you had a similar experience of abstinence teaching? Does putting it in the context of the whole gospel help you?

6
Porn and Pastoral Care

It was a lazy afternoon in mid-spring. Some friends and I were relaxing together in the living room after enjoying a good meal together. Talk turned to spiritual matters, and someone suggested that it would be good for us to tell each other our testimonies.

I was immediately quite nervous. Whenever I had told my story in the past, I'd conveniently left out my problems with porn. I'd been sure that if I was completely honest, people would judge me, and they wouldn't look at me the same way again. In this moment, I felt compelled to tell the whole truth. After allowing a few people to go before me while I gathered my composure, I then proceeded to tell my story, leaving nothing out.

My friends were stunned by what they heard. I was grateful that their reaction was not one of condemnation but appreciation for my honesty. I wasn't sure what I'd expected, but I hadn't expected that! I decided that day to be open and honest when telling my story.

I was very aware of my sin as I gave my testimony. Sin is a real concern for the Church, because we recognise that it separates us from God. There's no denying it, sin is a very real problem here. However, that can sometimes cause problems for Christians struggling with porn. In their hearts there's no doubt that what they're doing is sinful. It may take a while for them to stop enjoying the sin, though. That's part of what makes the cycle so hard to escape; as damaging as using porn is, in the moment it provides a release that's enjoyable. Once the porn user has reached a point where they're prepared to try to break the habit, they face an altogether different challenge.

The worst kind of sin?

On the whole, people in churches tend to feel uncomfortable discussing issues of a sexual nature. I've heard stories of Christian couples who sleep together before they're married, get pregnant and are ostracised by their church community when the truth comes out. Sometimes they're required to make a public apology, sometimes their indiscretion is announced from the platform. Even if that doesn't happen, there are the sidelong glances, the cold shoulders, and the feeling that everybody knows about their shame, which can make the church exactly the wrong place to facilitate any kind of redemption and recovery.

Porn creates the same kinds of reactions, although it seems to make people more uncomfortable than some other sexual sins. The reason for this is simple; people with porn habits tend to maintain those habits in secret for a long time before they're brought to light. When that happens, it shocks those who discover it, because they've been a part of this person's life for all this time and not known this very important thing about them.

In my first year of Bible college I was once again presented with the opportunity to share my story, this time in front of my class. We were each given ten minutes to share our testimony as an exercise in developing our communication skills. As I was preparing what I would say in the week before the class, I talked it through with someone very close to me. I was disappointed that this person tried to discourage me from being truthful about my experiences, because they were afraid my classmates might judge me or see me differently once they'd heard my story.

The way that people react to that first disclosure will play a vital part in how the porn user recovers. If their confession gets a condemnatory response, they will know that the shame they've been feeling is rightfully theirs, and embrace it. I use the word 'know' deliberately, because it won't feel like a case of mistakenly thinking that shame is their proper and permanent state. They will believe it with certainty, and once they have convinced themselves that they must remain ashamed and worthless because of what they've done, it's very difficult to convince them that they don't have to stay that way.

I'm not trying to condemn the Church here, but if I can gently challenge some of the prejudices we've picked up along the way I believe that the Church will become much more effective at caring for people who have been trapped by porn, and bringing them back into a healthy and grace-filled relationship with Christ. In Chapter 8 I will talk about how church leaders can change these prejudices through showing a better example. This isn't just for leaders, though. We all need to take our lead from Jesus, who confronted sin without a judgemental attitude. The best known instance of this is with the woman caught in adultery in John 8. Even people unfamiliar with the Bible would have heard the phrase: 'Whoever is without sin, let him cast the first stone.' It's almost become cliché, but let's not lose the revolutionary power behind Jesus' words.

My Bible college friend who sought to dissuade me from sharing my story said they had my best interests at heart. That might have been at least partly true, but it seemed to me that they felt ashamed for me, so they assumed others would too. I told my story to the class anyway, and received the same positive response I'd found in that small group of friends years earlier. It even led to some people deciding to address issues in their own lives as a result of what I'd said.

We should all take seriously Jesus' attitude of forgiveness rather than condemnation. I know that I sometimes have a tendency to feel superior when I see someone else's sinful behaviour. Being an imperfect human, I'm tempted to pass judgement on them, and that's every bit as shameful as the sin I've observed. Jesus demonstrates the incredible grace of God which is available to all of us who so desperately need it, regardless of how 'good' we think we are. It's out of that grace that we minister to those in the grip of porn.

This isn't about being a soft touch. Jesus certainly wasn't. I'm not suggesting that we ignore the sinful nature

82

of porn use in order to spare people's feelings. We should absolutely confront the sin, not in a way that demeans or denounces, but out of a desire to see people restored by Jesus. That means that we need to first offer grace, in the same way Jesus did, before giving the charge Jesus gave:

'Go now and leave your life of sin.'[1]

Recovery

Although God set me free from my addiction to porn, I spent years prior to that trying to sort out the problem myself. Even after I had been set free, I still struggled with lingering guilt and shame over what my life had been like. It took me a long time to understand and accept the fullness of what God had done for me in that moment; He had removed from me the guilt of my sin and taken away the shame of it as well.

Sometimes when we ask God to forgive our sins we can understand that He has done it because the Bible tells us that's what He'll do, but we take much longer to forgive ourselves.

As I've reflected on my own lack of forgiveness for myself, I've come to a sobering realisation. When we refuse to forgive ourselves, despite having asked God for forgiveness, we are inadvertently placing more importance upon the way we see ourselves than on the way God sees us. Paul writes:

God made him who had no sin to be sin for us, so that in him we might become the righteousness of God.[2]

Did you get that? If you are a Christian, you are forgiven by God through Jesus' sacrifice on the cross, and you now possess the righteousness of God. That means that when God looks at you He doesn't see your sin; He sees the righteousness of Jesus! If we truly believe this to be true - and we should – then what right do we have to refuse to forgive ourselves when God has forgiven us?

I realise that it's easy to say that we ought to forgive ourselves, but much harder to actually do it. It is vitally important when we're seeking to forgive ourselves that we ground that desire in what the Bible says about God's forgiveness of us. For me, that meant that I had to remind myself whenever I felt ashamed that I was already forgiven by God, and give those feelings back to God in prayer.

Recovering from porn addiction takes time. Like any kind of addiction recovery, it isn't easy, and shouldn't be attempted alone. Some people try to quit 'cold turkey', while others might try to gradually phase porn out of their lives. Neither of those approaches is particularly right or wrong; it comes down to each individual person.

Accountability

Meaningful accountability is vital to successful recovery from porn addiction. This will only work in the context of a trusting relationship, either with a spiritual leader or a close friend. Having a strong basis of trust is critical to create an atmosphere in which honesty is the norm. It helps if the 'leader' (for want of a better term) is willing to display some vulnerability so that the relationship doesn't feel one-sided.

You may be wondering why such a relationship is even necessary. After all, couldn't a porn addict simply pray and ask God to help them through it? I would never deny the power of prayer, especially given that my recovery experience came about through prayer in a moment, but my observations since have taught me that my story is not a common one.

When someone is sick, we pray for healing, but we also encourage them to go to their doctor. In the same way, I would always encourage a recovering porn addict to pray, but I'd also strongly advise an accountability relationship so that the recovery process isn't a solitary one. When it comes to recovering from porn addiction, there's much more to it than simply breaking the habit of watching porn. That's step one. The really hard work is in reshaping the person's character and repairing the damage done to their self-esteem.

Porn warps our perceptions of ourselves and of sex. It teaches us that we're unworthy of wholesome relationships; that we're dirty and unlovable, and that sex is just a physical action. This emotional trauma is very difficult to heal. Short of a miraculous intervention, it's virtually impossible to repair the damage done alone. This is where the accountability partner comes in.

Being an accountability partner is about more than just keeping tabs on your friend's internet usage. It goes beyond the occasional text to check that they haven't relapsed. The job of an accountability partner is to gently guide them through the pages of Scripture to rediscover who Jesus made them to be. At times it can seem like a huge responsibility, or even a burden, but I prefer to see it as a privilege. You get to be the one who leads a broken, hurting person who's been wrecked by porn back to a loving Father whose overwhelming desire is for them to be reunited with Him.

If you're reading this now and you've just begun this journey as someone's accountability partner, let that sense of privilege shape your attitude towards the process. If you've been an accountability partner for a while and you're feeling discouraged or burdened, I pray that this chapter helps to refocus you and that you're filled afresh with the grace of God by the power of the Holy Spirit to see your friend discover the freedom Christ offers.

If you're a porn user on the road to recovery, seek out someone on whom you can rely to be this person for you. If you've already found that person, make the decision to trust them, even when it's hard. Be completely honest with them. If you relapse, tell them. Accountability relationships are only effective if you're prepared to be fully honest. There may be times when they have to tell you things you don't want to hear, because you need to hear them. In those moments, remember why you trusted them to begin with. They have your best interests at heart. Recovering from porn addiction is hard. It requires perseverance and openness, but it is achievable. Believe that and let someone give you the help you need.

Breaking the habit

If you speak to anyone who's ever tried to free themselves from an addiction, whether it's smoking, narcotics, alcohol or even just caffeine, they'll have told you that it's not easy. There's a great deal of willpower required, so it can't be done if the addict hasn't first resolved of their own accord to stop. I'll concede that it could be possible to stop someone from viewing porn even if they don't want to, by simply limiting their access to it. However, that's not really achieving the goal, which is restoring the person, not simply removing the habit.

With that in mind, I'm going to direct this part of the chapter towards the recovering porn addict. After all, you're the one who stands to benefit most from this, and it's your decision to change which begins this process. First of all, well done for taking the first step! I hope that through reading this book up until now you've discovered that you're not a lost cause, and that this doesn't have to be a part of your life forever. Let's start with some practical tips for breaking the physical habit of watching porn. We'll get on to the emotional and spiritual recovery later.

Start by making a list of all the different media through which you view porn. You might have to think hard about this to make sure you don't miss any. To help you out, here's a list of possible media to which you may have access:

- Laptop/PC
- Tablet

- Smartphone

- Smart watch

- Television

- Games console

- Magazines

- e-book reader (porn can be text-based)

Once you've made your list, identify which of these devices can be protected against adult material. For instance, your laptop, tablet and smartphone can all be loaded with accountability software, which will keep track of your internet use. It's a good idea to ask your accountability partner to help you with this. Get them to set a password for your account that only they know, so that you can be protected from deactivating the software in a moment of temptation.

The next step is to limit your exposure to all of these media. These days it seems almost impossible to function without a smartphone, but it's helpful to try to keep your usage to public areas, or just the basics (calls, texts, etc) when you're alone. This is where you need to keep yourself accountable. If you're alone and feeling tempted to view porn, that's the moment to call your accountability partner.

Most instances of relapse with porn use tend to occur late at night. For that reason, I suggest that you don't take any of the devices you've listed to bed with you. If you use your smartphone as an alarm, consider buying a conventional alarm clock. Leave any potentially tempting devices in a completely separate room, so that you can't just turn over and pick them up to find some porn. It might seem a bit extreme. You might even think you'd never be tempted like that. You could be right, but is it worth the risk? Think about what you're trying to escape from, and what you're escaping to. It might be the precaution that seems silly to you now which saves you from falling back into old habits.

It takes real effort to break any habit. There is no guaranteed silver bullet which can deal with porn addiction so you don't have to do anything. It's possible that God might decide to set you free like he did me, but it is far more likely that your recovery will come through a process combining your own effort with the power of the Holy Spirit at work in your life.

The precautions you take to protect you from viewing porn will need to stay in place even when you no longer feel that you'll be tempted. When an alcoholic quits drinking, it's for life. They can't go back to the bottle even a little bit, because it doesn't take much to reopen the floodgates of addiction. The same is true of porn. Anyone who has previously struggled with porn addiction needs to remain vigilant, ruthlessly removing things from their life which might cause them to return to it.

If you think you're addicted to porn, I urge you to put into practice what you've read in this chapter. Find yourself an accountability partner and resolve between the two of you to do all you can to break your habit. Remember: it can be done!

Questions for reflection and discussion

1. Have other people's attitudes to porn prevented you from being open about your experiences? What would make you feel more able to speak up?

2. Is there someone in your life you're prepared to be completely honest with in an accountability relationship?

3. What practical steps can you take today to reduce potential temptation to look at porn?

7
Porn and the Mind

From time to time, my wife asks me a simple but difficult question: *What are you thinking about?* I'm not very good at answering that question. It's not that I don't think about anything – quite the opposite – but it seems that whenever I'm asked that question my mind goes blank! There are times when I'm thinking absolutely nothing, which is something my wife finds really difficult to understand.

I'm a very analytical person; I process everything internally. My thought life is very important because it's the primary way in which I help myself to understand the world around me. I like to take my time thinking about something before I speak or write about it. If I come across a new concept or idea, I might come back to it in my mind a few times over a period of hours or days while I figure it out.

I want to talk about an effect of porn use which doesn't get quite as much attention as some of the others. There are obvious effects of porn use: low self-worth, the need to watch porn in order to relax, self-centred sex drive, masturbation, secrecy and damaged relationships are just a few. The less obvious effect is how it changes our thought life.

Take a moment to think really carefully about your thought life. What do you think about on any given day? It might help you to make a list. Here's mine as an example, in no particular order.

- Food – what am I going to eat today?
- Work – what's on my to-do list and in which order should I do it?
- Energy levels – I'm tired/energised/stressed/busy/ excited today.
- What shall I post on social media today?
- I love my wife.
- What's on TV?
- How can I be more like Jesus and help others do the same?

I hope that wasn't too frightening an insight into my life! We all think about a variety of different things throughout the day. There might be a particular thing which dominates all the others. Let's call it your Primary Thought. Be really honest with yourself now – what is your Primary Thought?

Your Primary Thought will be the thought which carries the most importance in your mind. It might be something positive, like your love for a particular person. It could be something negative, like low self-worth. Your Primary

Thought will take up more of your thought life than anything else, and will therefore shape the way you behave and respond to situations day by day.

Captivated thoughts

We've talked already about how porn promises to fulfil our sexual desires. It's a solitary means to sexual pleasure without the heartache and difficulty of human relationship. It allows the user to consume all they want without giving anything in return. What porn also does is subtly override your Primary Thought, so that the most important thing to the user becomes their own sexual gratification. Once you've seen something it can't be unseen, and can be brought back to mind at the slightest provocation. This is why Paul writes:

> For though we live in the world, we do not wage war as the world does. The weapons we fight with are not the weapons of the world. On the contrary, they have divine power to demolish strongholds. We demolish arguments and every pretension that sets itself up against the knowledge of God, and we take captive every thought to make it obedient to Christ.[1]

The prospect of 'taking thoughts captive' can be a difficult one to get our heads around. How exactly are we supposed to do that? In some ways it comes down to willpower. There's self-discipline involved, so that we don't allow ourselves to dwell upon thoughts which are unhelpful. Thankfully, we have more than willpower on our side.

> The weapons we fight with are not the weapons of the world. On the contrary, they have divine power to demolish strongholds.

A Christian who is filled with the Holy Spirit has access to the weapons of the Spirit. These weapons, combined with a desire to purify our thought lives, can give us freedom from porn in our minds. When thoughts or images come into mind which are inappropriate, we can steel ourselves to ignore those thoughts, but we can also pray and draw on the Holy Spirit within us to take those thoughts captive.

I think Paul uses the metaphor of captivity deliberately here, because he wants to communicate to us that there is a finality to this action. A captive is locked up under guard, so that they cannot escape. They are out of sight, and out of mind. Each time we take a thought captive we take another step towards pure and godly thinking.

There is an often-quoted statistic which says that men think about sex on average once every seven seconds. I've always thought that was a bit far-fetched, so I felt vindicated to read a more accurate study which shows that 54 per cent of men think about sex every day or several times a day, 43 per cent a few times a week or a few times a month, and 4 per cent less than once a month.[2] Sex is not the Primary Thought for nearly half of the male population. I suspect that *What am I going to eat today?* might factor higher or more regularly for many men.

For the porn user, sex – or rather, their desire for an orgasm – is placed on a pedestal. They might not think about it every second of the day, but it can enter their minds with the slightest of stimuli. Everyday objects, situations and comments can trigger thoughts that lead to a person looking at porn the first opportunity they get. If that trigger happens early in a busy morning, it's possible that thoughts of the next available opportunity to watch porn will dominate the rest of the day, leaving them distracted, dissatisfied and even depressed.

When we talk about taking thoughts captive, there's a swap that needs to happen. People who are addicted to porn use are held captive by it. Their thoughts are captives to their sexual desires. That captivity needs turning on its head. We are set free from our captivity to sin by Jesus, and in the power He gives us we take sinful thoughts captive.

It isn't easy to break a habitual thought pattern once it's established. This is partly how porn use can become an addiction; it begins to dominate our thought life, even filling our subconscious thoughts. Breaking the physical habit of watching porn can be relatively easy, compared to changing the thought patterns that go along with it.

The Bible gives us a framework for combating unhelpful thought patterns:

> Do not be anxious about anything, but in every situation, by prayer and petition, with thanksgiving, present your requests to God. And the peace of God, which transcends all understanding, will guard your hearts and your minds in Christ Jesus.

Finally, brothers and sisters, *whatever is true, whatever is noble, whatever is right, whatever is pure, whatever is lovely, whatever is admirable – if anything is excellent or praiseworthy – think about such things.* Whatever you have learned or received or heard from me, or seen in me – put it into practice. And the God of peace will be with you.[3]

A number of years ago I was on a discipleship course. Part of what we did throughout the course was to study this passage in incredible depth. We looked at each of the words Paul uses in detail; we found out their roots in the Greek, looked at their synonyms and antonyms and considered what all that meant for our daily lives.

Perhaps that kind of study is a little too in-depth for most people – it might have been too in-depth for us too! Nevertheless, there is some mileage in considering the meaning of the words that Paul uses. What does it mean for you to think about what is true, what is noble?

Reclaiming your thought life

Prolonged use of pornography can change the way we think about sex, or even simply about the opposite sex. Someone who has never viewed porn might see someone of the opposite sex and think nothing out of the ordinary, while someone who has been (or still is) addicted to porn might find themselves plagued by questions such as, 'I wonder what she/he looks like naked?' or 'What would it be like to have sex with her/him?' This is the long-term effect of porn, which can be a battle for people long after they stop watching it. It is these thoughts which must be taken captive.

At times it may seem like the hold porn has on your life cannot be broken. There may be moments when you're tempted to give up hope of ever being free from it. Much like when someone gets a cold and quickly forgets what it's like to not have a cold, so too can we forget what it's like to live life without porn. Despite this, my encouragement to you is that it can be done. You can be free from porn. Submit your heart to God daily; allow the Holy Spirit to work in you, strengthening you and leading you; submit to an accountability relationship with someone and be completely honest with them. In time, by the grace of God, you can be free from porn.

I've talked before about protecting yourself from the effects of porn through eliminating things which bring temptation. I've recently had to remind myself to be ruthless with this.

At the time of writing, the film *Deadpool* is out in the cinemas. I'm a massive comic book geek and a big fan of Deadpool as a character. Naturally, I was excited when it was announced that they were going to make a *Deadpool* film, particularly because it gave Ryan Reynolds the opportunity to undo the damage that was done to the character in *X-Men Origins: Wolverine*.

Since I'm more than familiar with *Deadpool* from the comics, I fully expected the film to be violent. I didn't expect it to be too sexually explicit. When I read an early review of the film which mentioned some graphic sexual content, I ignored it. 'I doubt it's that bad,' I said to myself.

That was my first mistake. Any time you start convincing yourself that it'll be all right to watch something, that's a warning sign that maybe it won't be helpful for you.

I went to see *Deadpool* and really enjoyed it. I even posted a picture on my Instagram of myself wearing a *Deadpool* T-shirt as I was heading out to watch it. The next day, my senior pastor casually asked me how the film was. He then mentioned that he'd seen an article online about why Christians perhaps shouldn't go and see it. Initially I wrote it off, but as I reflected upon the brief conversation we'd had, I realised that the sexual content of the film had definitely stuck with me. I found myself lying in bed that night trying to banish images from the film from my mind so I could sleep.

I looked up the article and read it. It wasn't, as I expected, an attack on *Deadpool* as if it's the worst thing in the world. In fact, it wasn't about *Deadpool*, but about *Game of Thrones*; it had been reposted because it was relevant to *Deadpool* as well. It was actually very well written and made some reasonable and helpful points.[4]

As I lay there, I felt like a fool. I had convinced myself that I was immune from temptation because I have no desire to return to porn. Nobody is immune. It doesn't matter if you don't go back to looking at porn if the kinds of films or TV shows you're watching bring the same responses from you that porn used to. I was shocked at my own pride; I knew that I had to make this right immediately. I prayed a simple prayer and committed before God to be more ruthless with what I allow myself to watch.

Being ruthless in this way can be a real sacrifice. It might seem like a silly example to those who aren't huge comic book geeks like me, but there's already talk of a *Deadpool* sequel. I won't be going to see it. I won't be buying the DVD, which means that my superhero collection won't be complete. Being something of a completionist, this is probably a bigger deal to me than to many.

If we're not willing to sacrifice even those things which are so insignificant compared to the damage porn does to us, we stand little chance of redeeming our thought lives from the effects of porn.

Don't be tempted to think 'it's not that bad', as I did. No film or TV show is so good that it's worth losing yourself to watch it.

> Whatever is true, whatever is noble, whatever is right, whatever is pure, whatever is lovely, whatever is admirable – if anything is excellent or praiseworthy – think about such things.[5]

Questions for reflection and discussion

1. What do you regularly think about on an average day? Make a list, and use it to identify your Primary Thought.

2. What effect does porn have on your thought life?

3. What practical step can you take today to begin to take captive any unhelpful thoughts?

8
Porn and the Church

Sex has long been an uncomfortable topic. Parents both inside and outside the Church struggle to talk to their children about it; hence, daft stories like the birds and the bees.

It seems to me that people in the Church are some of the least comfortable with discussing issues of sex and sexuality. It is generally accepted (and rightly so) that sex is something that only married people should be doing so, too often that has been the extent of any conversation in church about sex. The discomfort then extends towards those who overstep that boundary and have sex outside marriage. I find it incredibly sad that for so long our first response to someone confessing premarital sex has been awkward silence mixed with condemnation. Don't misunderstand me here, I'm not in any way condoning premarital sex or extramarital affairs. By the same token, though, I think it's high time we started forcing our way through our institutional awkwardness about sex, so that those who struggle with it can get the support they need.

None of us is perfect. Nobody can claim to be completely 'pure' – even if you've never had any issues with sex, you're still human and therefore prone to sin. What was it Jesus said about casting the first stone?

I'm being deliberately direct here, because I want to challenge anyone who looks down in judgement on people who confess porn use or anything similar. I can understand if it makes you feel uncomfortable. You can be sure that it's not exactly easy for the person confessing to you, either! In fact, the sheer fact that they're confessing to you is in itself a miracle. They've probably been struggling for a long time, living in shame, trying to work up the courage to talk to someone about what they're going through so they can get some help.

Imagine being so ashamed of something you've done that you've come to believe that you're completely worthless and past redemption; the weight of your sin is so heavy that you can't imagine ever being free of it, but still there's a slight hope inside you that if you could tell just one person, maybe they'd be able to help you. Maybe they'd show you a kindness you're sure you don't deserve, and you'll find the freedom that you can only dream of. Imagine instead that when you tell that person they respond with judgement, affirming all that you've already come to believe about yourself. This isn't just about sexual sin; we need to stop offering people judgement in exchange for their confession, but show them Jesus and His incredible saving grace.

If you recognised yourself even in a small way there, please don't ignore it. Be annoyed at me if you like, but please also pray. Ask God to reveal to you if you have judgement in your heart, and to replace it with his grace.

Vulnerability

Vulnerability is one of the most important qualities a church community can have. I love the Church. There's no other group of people in the world so diverse and weird in their own ways, and yet so united around a central world view. We have the opportunity, and a responsibility, to be truly vulnerable with one another, so that together we can grow to be more like Jesus.

I think we're only recently coming to understand just how valuable vulnerability is. For a long time, church has been a place where you have to pretend that you're the holiest you can possibly be, while on the inside you feel quite the opposite. It's been a place of competition, where we all battle it out to see who is the most spiritual. We even sometimes have the cheek to read the Gospels and scoff at the disciples for not having enough faith (as if we, in the same situations, would behave perfectly and believe fully)! In the last couple of decades or so, the Church has been on a journey to rediscover the value of vulnerability.

I've heard it said that a pastor should never show weakness to their congregation. The thinking behind that is that it would somehow weaken their position, and the congregation's trust in their pastor would be shaken. Nothing could be further from the truth!

That mindset comes from a profound misunderstanding of vulnerability. It assumes that showing yourself to be weak is an action of weakness. I don't believe that. Allowing other people to see your vulnerability is an incredible feat of strength. It goes against our survival instinct, and our internal sense of insecurity. We worry that if people see just how weak we are they'll never respect us, but in reality, when a pastor is willing to show that they are just as human as their congregation, the congregation feel much more inclined to trust their pastor. More importantly, the congregation feel liberated in their own humanity, and therefore able to reveal their own vulnerability in order to grow.

Jesus Himself modelled this way of leading. When His disciples argued among themselves about who should be greater, He gave this famous response:

> You know that the rulers of the Gentiles lord it over them, and their high officials exercise authority over them. Not so with you. Instead, whoever wants to become great among you must be your servant, and whoever wants to be first must be your slave – just as the Son of Man did not come to be served, but to serve, and to give his life as a ransom for many.[1]

Before his final meal with His disciples, Jesus washed their feet. It can be hard for us to understand how radical this was. We are well used to washing our own feet, which don't even get that dirty if we're wearing shoes. Of course, that doesn't mean any of us is that keen to go anywhere near anyone else's feet. At least on that level we can see that for Jesus as a leader to wash His followers' feet was an astonishing display of vulnerability. In the days when Jesus was walking this earth, people wore open-toed sandals. In a pre-tarmac world, there would have been a lot of dust and sand on the road, so by the end of the day everyone's feet would be disgustingly dirty. Therefore, the washing of feet before a meal was a task given to the lowest of household servants. It certainly wasn't something that was ever done by a rabbi – a religious teacher – such as Jesus!

> When he had finished washing their feet, he put on his clothes and returned to his place. 'Do you understand what I have done for you?' he asked them. 'You call me "Teacher" and "Lord", and rightly so, for that is what I am. Now that I, your Lord and Teacher, have washed your feet, you also should wash one another's feet. I have set you an example that you should do as I have done for you. Very truly I tell you, no servant is greater than his master, nor is a messenger greater than the one who sent him. Now that you know these things, you will be blessed if you do them.'[2]

I have found that when I've told my story to groups of people, it has been an effort on my part to allow myself to be vulnerable. Nevertheless, the pay-off has been obvious. People have come to me afterwards to seek help with overcoming porn addiction; others have come to thank me for being willing to be so open. Even if people don't struggle with porn, they have been grateful to know that their pastor is prepared to be vulnerable with them.

We have to get away from nature's idea of 'survival of the fittest'. There's no such thing in Jesus' Church.

But God chose the foolish things of the world to shame the wise; God chose the weak things of the world to shame the strong.[3]

God desires honesty from us, not just in our relationship with Him, but in the way we relate to one another as well.

So what does all of this have to do with porn?

Simply put, we need to create a culture of vulnerability in our churches, so that people who are struggling with porn know that they are in a safe place to seek help. Without this assurance, many people will continue in silent shame, never fully knowing the grace of Christ and the freedom that goes with it.

'You go first'

It all starts with pastors. As the people whose responsibility it is to oversee the spiritual development of the local church, they (and I count myself in that 'they') have a crucial role to play in shaping that culture of honest vulnerability. In part, that's why I'm writing this book. More than that, though, I made a commitment between myself and God a few years ago to be honest when I'm asked about how I became a Christian. It'd be easy for me to gloss over my past issues with porn, but I know that if I'd heard my pastor (or someone in leadership over me in any other capacity) confess something like that while I was going through it, I'd have felt encouraged to talk to that leader and get help.

Maybe you're a pastor who's never had any issue with porn. Maybe sexual sin in any form has never been a problem for you. Thank God for you! You don't have to have struggled with the exact issues your congregation are going through to show that you're a vulnerable human too. You don't have to confess a past struggle with porn. What you do have to do is be prepared to open your life a little from the platform, so that your congregation can better relate to you and themselves. It's a big responsibility, but I imagine you knew that would be the case when you started out in ministry.

It can be surprising how many people in churches really seem to think their pastor is or should be perfect. 'But you're not like the rest of us, are you, pastor?' and comments like it are said more often than you'd think.

One of the hot topics for church leaders these days is culture. I can't claim to be an expert on shaping culture in churches, but it doesn't take one to know that changing the culture of a church takes time, and has to start from the top. You can't expect the church to become comfortable with vulnerability overnight. It will probably take longer than you'd like it to. Even so, it's important to keep setting the example.

Creating a culture of vulnerability doesn't have to come through large-scale confessions of past sins. The most helpful thing is to preach consistently in a manner which makes it clear that the contents of your message are as applicable to you as to your congregation. We are all human beings, inherently flawed and daily in need of the grace of God. To pretend otherwise puts the preacher in danger of pride, as well as potentially alienating members of their congregation who come to believe they could never live up to the spiritual example of their pastor.

The Bible is clear that none of us is worthy or good enough to come before God in and of ourselves.[4] Therefore, none of us has the right to condemn anyone else for their sin. It is beholden upon church leaders, then, to show the example in the way they lead and preach, of what it looks like to live in the freedom of the gospel, with no condemnation.[5]

Pastor, take an honest look at your heart and your ministry. Is there anything in your conduct or preaching which could lead anyone to feel condemned for their sin rather than leading them into the loving embrace of their heavenly Father? Have you, knowingly or unknowingly, responded with condemnation or judgement when someone confessed to you their struggles with pornography?

That last question applies to all Christians, pastor or not. Don't move on from this chapter without going before God in repentance and receiving His grace.

Questions for reflection and discussion

1. Is the culture in your church open to vulnerability? If not, what can be done to start to change it?

2. Have you encountered leaders who show a good example of vulnerability? Has this made you feel more able to be open about your own struggles?

3. Refer back to the questions at the end of the chapter. Does anything need to change in you?

9
Sex in the Bible

Sex is the most intimate thing one person can do with another. It involves not just their bodies, but their whole selves. When two people have sex, they open themselves to one another on a level which goes beyond the physical. That is why promiscuity can be so damaging. The notion of 'casual sex' is a misnomer which sadly claims many victims. Porn plays a role in warping our view of sex, both through its casual nature and its portrayal of a kind of sex which is not replicated in a healthy sexual relationship.

Through watching porn, I was exposed to a world in which women are merely vessels for fulfilling a man's sexual desire. The kind of sex portrayed in porn shows little regard for the woman's sexual fulfilment, and leads male viewers to assume that they can always have sex the way they like, and their partner will just enjoy it. A truly loving sexual relationship requires both partners to seek first and foremost to serve the other, rather than themselves.

Since porn can lead us to have such an unhelpful view of sex, it is important that we understand the purpose for which sex was created. To do that, we need to open up the Bible.

Before I start, let me just say that this will not be a comprehensive treatise on everything the Bible has to say about sex. I'd have to write several separate books for that! I'm going to focus on some key areas which help us to understand God's purpose for sex, in order to also discover where porn fits with Scripture.

The Old Testament

The Old Testament has quite a lot to say about sex. There are laws prohibiting sex with relatives or animals,[1] laws requiring men who sleep with unmarried women to marry them,[2] and even laws about lying about your virginity.[3] While I would never want to write off these things, it is important not to focus merely on the commandments of the Law of Moses, since many others of these commandments are no longer upheld by Christians owing to them having been fulfilled by Jesus.[4]

Jesus came to fulfil the ceremonial law which required the people to sacrifice animals in order to gain forgiveness for their sins, but He upheld the moral law which shows us God's moral standard for His people. The commands in the Law of Moses show us God's desire for His people to be distinct from the other cultures surrounding them, and to be set apart as holy for Him. Some of these laws are reaffirmed in Jesus' teachings and elsewhere in the New Testament, which is why they are still followed by

112

Christians today. It's really important that we understand the context for which each book of the Bible was written, in order to make sure we interpret Scripture effectively. Many people misunderstand the relationship between the Old and New Testaments because they haven't grasped the contexts for which each book was written. As important as that is, that's not what this book is about. For now, let's talk about the Song of Solomon.

Song of Solomon

There is a lot of debate about the proper way to interpret the Song of Solomon. Some say that it was written as an allegory for the relationship between God and Israel, while others say that it is a prophetic book about Christ and the Church. I understand where both of those interpretations are coming from, but I find it more plausible to take the book at face value, as a collection of poems describing the romantic relationship between a man and a woman, culminating in their marriage. After all, romantic relationships are a large part of life as a human being, so why wouldn't the Bible include something about how it feels to be in such a relationship?

The Song of Solomon follows the romance between a couple as they begin exploring their feelings for one another. The way that they talk to one another makes it clear that it is perfectly natural and biblically sanctioned for a couple to desire one another.

There has been a misconception in the past that because the Bible prohibits sex before marriage that means that Christian couples can't enjoy one another until that point.

Some couples go too far the other way as well. They assume that it is simply the act of sexual intercourse which is considered to be sinful outside marriage, so therefore they do everything *except* have sex. This is completely missing the point. The Bible's stance on premarital relations is not simply about stopping unmarried couples from having sex. God created sex for two reasons: pleasure and procreation (Genesis 1:28). Both of these were intended to happen within the context of marriage.

The Song of Solomon has a refrain running through it which says 'do not arouse or awaken love until it so desires'.[5] The point of this refrain is that there is a proper way for a romantic relationship to progress. To rush straight to sex is to miss out several key elements which go together to build a healthy relationship. Sadly, the custom of our culture is for sex to happen as part of getting to know one another; it is not considered something to save until marriage.

God created sex for our pleasure. The Song of Solomon illustrates this by giving us access to the thoughts of the two lovers about each other. Neither of them are shy about voicing their feelings for one another:

> Your neck is like the tower of David,
> built with courses of stone;
> on it hang a thousand shields,
> all of them shields of warriors.
> Your breasts are like two fawns,
> like twin fawns of a gazelle
> that browse among the lilies.
> Until the day breaks

and the shadows flee,
I will go to the mountain of myrrh
and to the hill of incense.
You are altogether beautiful, my darling;
there is no flaw in you.[6]

His cheeks are like beds of spice
yielding perfume.
His lips are like lilies
dripping with myrrh.
His arms are rods of gold
set with topaz.
His body is like polished ivory
decorated with lapis lazuli.
His legs are pillars of marble
set on bases of pure gold.
His appearance is like Lebanon,
choice as its cedars.
His mouth is sweetness itself;
he is altogether lovely.[7]

Obviously this is not how we would talk about someone we fancy these days! Even so, if we decipher the poetic language, it's clear that these two had a strong desire for one another. Even though they waited to fulfil those desires until they were married, they felt no need to stifle their feelings in the meantime. Having sexual desires is part of who we are, and completely natural. In fact, it's a good gift from God! However, as much as our culture and media try to convince us otherwise, it is not the be-all and end-all.

We've talked already about the way that porn presents sex. What's really clear from the Song of Solomon is that God's purpose for sex is far removed from how it is now seen in our society. Sex is a precious thing, which is deeply valued by God and should therefore be deeply valued by us. Sex is most definitely to be enjoyed, but not as a commodity or simply a casual pastime. When sex is kept exclusively between a husband and wife, it is as fulfilling as it can be.

> He who finds a wife finds what is good and receives favour from the Lord.[8]

The New Testament

My focus for a New Testament understanding of sex is 1 Corinthians. Paul writes to the church in Corinth, a metropolitan city which served as a nexus of trade for the Roman Empire. Because of its trade links, Corinth was a mixing pot of cultures and religions. The prevailing lifestyle seemed to be hedonism – the pursuit of pleasure. Temples to the Greek gods were staffed by prostitutes, with whom a person could have sex in order to enquire of the gods. Although marriages were mainly monogamous, there was no concept of absolute sexual morality. Sexual standards for women were set by the men. This was framed as 'honouring' the women, but in reality the men simply had control over what was sexually acceptable for women and what wasn't, while there were no such rules for the men. These confused ideas about sex (among other church issues) led Paul to write this letter.

Paul uses very strong language when he writes to the Corinthians, because he is aware of some serious incidences of sexual sin in the church. This is what he says:

> I wrote to you in my letter not to associate with sexually immoral people — not at all meaning the people of this world who are immoral, or the greedy and swindlers, or idolaters. In that case you would have to leave this world. But now I am writing to you that you must not associate with anyone who claims to be a brother or sister but is sexually immoral or greedy, an idolater or slanderer, a drunkard or swindler. Do not even eat with such people.[9]

Paul makes a clear distinction between the activity of those inside the church and those outside. He doesn't suggest that the church try to change the behaviour of people who aren't part of the church; he takes it as read that their sexual ethics will be different. However, he is very strong on sexual ethics within the church, commanding the church to not even associate with people who say they are believers and yet are sexually immoral!

This might seem a bit harsh to us today. Paul's main objective in writing this is to make sure that the church doesn't give the appearance of glorifying sinful behaviour. He doesn't limit this simply to sexual misconduct, although he is clear that the behaviour in question is sinful. He elaborates on this more in chapter 6:

> 'I have the right to do anything,' you say – but not everything is beneficial. 'I have the right to do

anything' – but I will not be mastered by anything. You say, 'Food for the stomach and the stomach for food, and God will destroy them both.' The body, however, is not meant for sexual immorality but for the Lord, and the Lord for the body. By his power God raised the Lord from the dead, and he will raise us also. Do you not know that your bodies are members of Christ himself? Shall I then take the members of Christ and unite them with a prostitute? Never! Do you not know that he who unites himself with a prostitute is one with her in body? For it is said, 'The two will become one flesh.' But whoever is united with the Lord is one with him in spirit.

Flee from sexual immorality. All other sins a person commits are outside the body, but whoever sins sexually, sins against their own body. Do you not know that your bodies are temples of the Holy Spirit, who is in you, whom you have received from God? You are not your own; you were bought at a price. Therefore honour God with your bodies.[10]

Commentators suggest that the phrase 'I have the right to do anything' was a Corinthian slogan of sorts. Paul seems to be quoting it because the Corinthian church had adopted it for themselves; they were using it as licence to behave however they liked. The trouble with this is that the Church was always supposed to be countercultural. If there are things which people in the Church are doing because people outside the Church are doing them, then there is a problem. That is why Paul adds the second part, '… but not everything is beneficial'.

Sex outside marriage is the norm in our culture. It's strange to most people who aren't connected to church that Christians don't have sex before they are married. For some people, it's perfectly all right to have a one-night stand. For others that isn't OK, but it's normal to have sex when you're in a dating relationship with someone. I've heard some Christians suggest that it's all right for a couple to sleep together, as long as they love each other and they are intending to marry. While this is a common viewpoint in our society, it does not have a basis in Scripture.

What many people do not understand is that there is more to sex than the physical. There is a spiritual component to sex, whereby the couple become 'one', as I have already touched upon. This is why the Bible talks about a married couple becoming 'one flesh'. Notice that Paul doesn't just tell us to *avoid* sexual immorality, he tells us to *flee* from it!

Paul quotes another Corinthian phrase, 'Food for the stomach and the stomach for food'. We could understand this as 'Sex for the body, and the body for sex', which is a common idea today. Sex feels good, so we should be allowed to do it with whomever we like. While that may be what many non-Christians believe, it certainly isn't what God intends for people who profess to be following Him. This is why Paul adds, 'The body, however, is not meant for sexual immorality but for the Lord, and the Lord for the body.' Our bodies are meant for far more than just sex. Don't get me wrong: sex is great, but it doesn't provide for us what God does.

What, then, does Paul have to say about how sexual relationships *should* be conducted? He goes on in chapter 7:

Now for the matters you wrote about: 'It is good for a man not to have sexual relations with a woman.' But since sexual immorality is occurring, each man should have sexual relations with his own wife, and each woman with her own husband. The husband should fulfil his marital duty to his wife, and likewise the wife to her husband. The wife does not have authority over her own body but yields it to her husband. In the same way, the husband does not have authority over his own body but yields it to his wife. Do not deprive each other except perhaps by mutual consent and for a time, so that you may devote yourselves to prayer. Then come together again so that Satan will not tempt you because of your lack of self-control. I say this as a concession, not as a command. I wish that all of you were as I am. But each of you has your own gift from God; one has this gift, another has that.

Now to the unmarried and the widows I say: it is good for them to stay unmarried, as I do. But if they cannot control themselves, they should marry, for it is better to marry than to burn with passion.[11]

Here, Paul is addressing a question about which the Corinthians had written to him. It appears that some of them had gone to the opposite extreme, assuming that all kinds of sexual activity are sinful and should therefore be avoided. From Paul's response, it is clear that this is just not true! While Paul does say that he'd prefer for everyone to stay single as he is (for the sake of greater ministry opportunities), the way he talks about the marital relationship makes it clear that sex is in fact a very good thing. We all have sexual desires, but the proper context for them to be fulfilled is within marriage. There is no hint within Paul's writings of an appropriate sexual relationship between an unmarried couple; if the couple want to have sex, they must first get married.

The heart of the matter

When I was in school I had a female friend who wasn't a Christian. She had a couple of boyfriends during the time I knew her, and was very open with me about sex. She knew I was a Christian and couldn't get her head around the fact that I was a virgin on purpose. She said to me one day, 'I just couldn't live without sex – I don't know how you manage it!'

The prevailing attitude in society is that sex is one of the most important things in life. As I have said before in this book, in reality, sex is not the be-all and end-all of life; it's great, but not the pinnacle of human experience. For the Christian, the purpose of life is to become more like Jesus. If this is our goal, our attitude towards sex will be vastly different from the rest of society.

I have already mentioned abstinence. Abstinence has been the teaching of the Church throughout its history, and for good reason. However, I prefer to emphasise purity, out of a desire to please God. The problem many people have had with abstinence teaching is that they saw it as a draconian set of rules with no relevance to the present. But for Christians, any rules which we follow have their basis in our relationship with Jesus. If you have no relationship with Jesus, you have no reason to want to keep yourself sexually pure. If you do have a relationship with Jesus, every area of your life is submitted to Him, including your sex life. Christians should be so captivated by Jesus that being more like Him is the foremost desire in their heart.

As we have seen here, the Bible has a lot to say about sex. Though it makes no mention of pornography, it is clear that God's intention for sex was never for us to watch others doing it. The Bible tells us that sex is to be enjoyed within marriage because that really is the best setting for this most intimate of acts. Anything short of this is missing the point. The good news is that nobody is beyond redemption. If you're struggling with porn addiction and wondering if it will ruin your future (or current) marital sex life, you can have hope, because it doesn't have to. If you, with the help of the Holy Spirit and a trusted friend, can eliminate porn use from your life, you can go on to enjoy a healthy and godly sex life with your spouse. If you're already married and struggling with porn, you too can turn this around. It may take a long time to regain your spouse's trust and restore your sex life, but stick at it – it'll be worth it in the end!

A note on culture

There has been a theme in this chapter – that of the interplay between our secular culture and Scripture. We are living in unprecedented times. It can no longer be said that the morality of our society is drawn from the Bible. In fact, for some people it is something to celebrate that the prevailing view is that the Bible is not authoritative.

We face a great challenge in this generation and the generations to come, as to how we communicate the truth of the Bible, especially to people who come to faith in Jesus from a non-Christian background. If the prevailing view of our culture is that the Bible is outdated, particularly in the area of sexual ethics, it may be difficult for new Christians to accept the authority of Scripture on these issues. Even within the Church, attitudes of young people towards sex may be shaped more by social media than by Scripture.

We must be wholly committed to discipleship – to helping people become who Jesus would be if he were them, as Dallas Willard once put it.[12] Our priority must be pointing people to Jesus as the focus of their life and faith. Discipleship shapes us into the likeness of Jesus in every area of our lives. My strong conviction is that the way we view and interact with our culture must be shaped by Scripture, and not the other way around. This comes through closely following Jesus in discipleship.

Questions for reflection and discussion

1. What was your view of the Bible's position on sex? Did anything in this chapter surprise you?

2. What does it mean for you to be pure? How would that be possible?

3. Has your viewpoint on sex been shaped more by the culture you live in than by Scripture?

10
Masturbation

As I told you at the start of this book, when I was growing up, my family and I attended a nice Anglican church. We'd settled there after moving into the town when I was seven, because of a friend I met at school who went there. It was a proper 'family' church, where everybody knew everybody.

During my mid-teens, I remember my friend coming to me once before the church service. She had a copy of a well-known book about relationships, and she looked troubled by it. She opened the book to a particular page and handed it to me. It was the chapter about masturbation. After a little while, she said to me, 'Christian boys don't really do that, do they?'

I felt very awkward. This was right in the middle of my years of porn use, so masturbation was most definitely a thing that I did. I didn't have the courage to be honest with my friend, so I told her that Christian boys didn't do that sort of thing. If my friend is reading this, I'm sorry I lied to you.

Not long after that incident, I went to a seminar on relationships, which was being led by a well-known Christian speaker. The question was raised about whether or not masturbation was OK for a Christian, and the speaker's response has puzzled me since. My recollection is that he said masturbation is fine, if it is done without any impure thoughts. I'm not completely sure that's what the speaker was trying to communicate to us, but what I took away from the seminar as a teenage boy was that I could masturbate as much as I liked, as long as I didn't think anything impure while I was doing it.

It should be no surprise that a teenage boy heard a comment like that and took it as licence to continue doing what he'd previously assumed was wrong. On reflection, I wonder if the speaker's point was that it *would be* OK to masturbate *if it were possible* to have no impure thoughts while doing so – the suggestion being that such a thing is not possible. Either way, I don't agree with the point the speaker was making.

It is true that masturbation is more often than not accompanied by impure thoughts or images. However, even if those thoughts and images were removed, it wouldn't make masturbation a healthy habit.

Spilled seed and selfish sex

Masturbation is, in and of itself, selfish. Our sexual desires are a gift given to us by God to be enjoyed in the most intimate of relationships – marriage. Solitary sex was not part of God's design.

There's a story in the Old Testament which is often quoted as proof that masturbation is sinful. It is found in Genesis 38.

The story is quite a complicated one, which requires some insight into the culture of the time in order to understand. Judah has three sons. Er, one of his sons, gets married, but dies before he can father any children. In accordance with the ancient Hebrew custom of 'levirate marriage', Er's brother was required to sleep with his widow so that she would become pregnant. The child would be considered to be Er's, so that his family line continued despite his death.[1]

The key verses I've heard quoted in the context of masturbation are verses 9-10:

> But Onan knew that the child would not be his; so whenever he slept with his brother's wife, he spilled his semen on the ground to avoid providing offspring for his brother. What he did was wicked in the Lord's sight; so the Lord put him to death also.

The phrase 'spilled his semen on the ground', along with the extreme response from the Lord, has given grounds for calling masturbation a sin. However, although the conclusion is correct, the means of getting there is not. Onan's sin wasn't simply that he 'spilled his semen on the ground', but that he refused to father a child on behalf of his brother. Onan knew that if his brother were to have a legal heir, that heir would receive a share of inheritance which otherwise would go to Onan himself.

Onan had a duty, according to the law and culture of the time, to provide a son for his brother. In his selfishness, he disobeyed. Notice that the only part of the law he disobeyed was the part which required him to actually father a child. He was perfectly happy to have sex with his brother's widow. That part was enjoyable for him, and he probably thought he could give the appearance of obeying and claim that there was some problem with her which meant she wasn't becoming pregnant. When one partner is selfish in sex, it cheapens the whole thing. To Onan, his brother's widow was either a legal obligation or an opportunity for an orgasm, or both. There is no sense in which he honoured her or his brother in this situation, and it cost him dearly.

Often, with issues like masturbation, we like to find a 'proof text' to tell us definitively whether it is right or wrong. Onan's sin has been used as a proof text, but its context shows that it has very little relevance to masturbation.

Unfortunately, there is no verse in the Bible which clearly says 'masturbation is wrong' or 'masturbation is right'. Therefore, we need to ask different questions of the Bible to come to a conclusion on this issue.

What is right or wrong?

Life is simpler when we can deal in black and white, but often we face grey areas. We ask questions such as 'Is masturbation sinful?' and hope that we can find a clear 'yes' or 'no' answer. I'm sure there are some who would immediately give one of those two answers as if it should be obvious, but find themselves in difficulty when they are asked why they have been so confident in their answer.

Not too many years ago, masturbation was generally understood to be sinful, and there was little argument about it. It is still an uncomfortable topic for many people, particularly in Christian circles, which means that having a robust discussion about it can be difficult.

For some people, masturbation would be included within the general category of 'sexual immorality' which is clearly presented as sinful throughout the Bible. [2] The difficulty with this is that the Bible doesn't make a list of things which are classed as 'sexual immorality'. This is most likely because the original readers would have needed no such list to know what the writer was referring to. However, our modern society has been through several definitions of sexual immorality, so if masturbation is to be included in that category it needs to be justified as to why.

Even during the height of my time using porn, I had no doubt that what I was doing was sexually immoral. Masturbation was, of course, part of that. My feelings around this most likely stemmed from my Christian upbringing. I had never considered the Bible to be anything other than authoritative, so I didn't question the idea that masturbation would be classed as sexual immorality. The overriding feeling this produced within me was guilt.

Guilt can motivate us to do good things. It can lead someone to apologise for a wrong they've done, and make amends to the person they wronged. However, guilt is not a good motivator, because at its heart it is burdensome. When someone does something primarily motivated by guilt, they rarely feel good about it. This was my experience with trying to eliminate masturbation from my life. I knew it was wrong, so I felt guilty for doing it. I tried to stop, but every time I failed I felt more guilty.

Even if we can clearly present a biblical case for masturbation being included in the list of 'sexual immorality', it is still unlikely to lead someone for whom masturbation is a habit to decide to break that habit with a positive attitude.

It's all about Jesus, really

Your approach to the issue of masturbation will depend largely upon whether or not you are a follower of Jesus. If you aren't, then the idea that masturbation is sinful may hold very little weight for you. After all, there are plenty of people who are also not followers of Jesus who think masturbation is not only fine, but healthy.

If you are a follower of Jesus, your moral standard has to be different. Issues like masturbation can tie people in knots, especially if they are trying to justify a black-and white-position on it. The common question would be, 'Where in the Bible does it say that masturbation is sinful?'

When someone asks this question, they are rarely satisfied with anything other than an explicit sentence in the Bible which says something like 'Thou shalt not masturbate'. Since no such sentence exists in the Bible, it is hard to give an adequate answer to such questions.

For Christians, the Bible is our authority in life.[3] It isn't simply a rule book, but it does govern our morality because it shows us what God is like and in turn what He wants His followers to be like. Therefore, if there are things which are considered to be moral grey areas, our attitude should not be to prove that these things are sinful; if we can't prove from the Bible that something is *not* sinful, then it is something we should avoid.

Our focus should not be on simply discovering whether or not masturbation is sinful. It is far more important to discover if masturbation is *holy*.

Jesus said, 'Be perfect, therefore, as your heavenly Father is perfect.'[4] That's a high moral standard! I wonder how often as Christians we forget this and allow ourselves to ignore habits which don't match up to what Jesus is asking of us.

There's an obvious response here: 'How can I possibly be perfect?' Good question. There has only ever been one perfect person – Jesus. Everyone else falls woefully short. So why does Jesus tell us to be perfect? Leon Morris gives a good answer:

> To set this kind of perfection before his followers means that Jesus saw them as always having something for which to strive. No matter how far along the path of Christian service we are, there is still something to aim for. There is a wholeheartedness about being Christian; all that we have and all that we are must be taken up into the service of the Father.[5]

Following Jesus is all-encompassing. If you're a Christian, there should be no part of your life which is not submitted to Jesus. We are all on a journey in this, because in reality there will be things which we have subconsciously held back – things which we haven't yet surrendered to Jesus, whether we know it or not. When we understand that this Christian life is not segmented, but Jesus is interested in every part of it, our perspective on such issues masturbation should change. In all of this, it's important to recognise that, although following Jesus involves some effort on our part, it's not through any of our striving that we become like Jesus – that's the work of the Holy Spirit.

During my years of struggling with porn, I didn't understand this. Although I was aware of the sinfulness of what I was doing, I didn't know that Jesus was interested in even those 'dirty' or 'shameful' parts of my life, and He wanted to remake them into something holy and pleasing to Him.

This is a process which all of us are going through from the point at which we decide to follow Jesus. The fancy theological word for it is 'sanctification'. It means 'setting apart', and it describes this gradual process through which a person is changed by the Holy Spirit to look more like Jesus. As Paul writes, 'we all, who with unveiled faces contemplate the Lord's glory, are being transformed into his image with ever-increasing glory, which comes from the Lord, who is the Spirit'.[6]

Did you get what that means? The pressure is off! We are aiming for Jesus' high moral standard of perfection, but we aren't required to do it on our own or entirely of our own effort. We are being transformed by the Holy Spirit, with 'ever-increasing glory' – gradual steps – to become more like Jesus, who is perfect.[7]

In terms of masturbation, here's what this all means. The issue is not about whether or not it is sinful; it is about whether or not is it holy. Does masturbation help you to become more like Jesus? Does it please God?

Too much of our focus is on sin, which is negative. When we think this way, it affects the way we see ourselves and the way we see God. We should be aware of our sin, because otherwise we'll continue in ignorance. Confession of sin is a good and biblical thing to do, both to God and to other trusted Christians.[8] However, when our approach is focused upon the sin itself, we come before God as 'a sinner' and we see God as a disciplinarian. But if we change our mindset and instead focus on how to please God, we can come before Him as His children, knowing that He is our loving Father who forgives us.

How you see yourself is important. If you see yourself as a sinner, then it is likely guilt will be your constant companion. If you see yourself as a child of God, then you know He loves you in spite of your sin and you can receive His forgiveness freely and move on. There will be times when you will slip up. It happens. You get to choose how you respond in those situations. R T Kendall says, 'God wants you to close the time gap between sin and repentance.'[9]

That means when you slip up, don't dwell on it. Don't beat yourself up about it; deal with it. You'll probably feel as if you can't possibly come before God right after you've done *that*, but that's a lie. The moment you realise that you've done, thought or said something that doesn't please God, you can bring it before Him in repentance and receive His forgiveness immediately.

We often leave a time gap between sin and repentance because we feel we don't deserve to be forgiven so quickly. We're right to believe that – in fact, we don't deserve to be forgiven at all! This is what the Bible calls 'grace' – getting what we don't deserve. Thankfully, we don't get to decide what we deserve to receive from God. That's entirely His prerogative, and He has chosen grace. It's a gift, which means it's free. Take it!

Questions for reflection and discussion

1. Have you ever been asked what the Bible says about masturbation? How did you respond?

2. How will approaching the issue of masturbation in terms of pleasing God change your perspective on it?

3. What steps can you put in place to guard yourself from continuing habits which don't please God?

11
Conclusion

As I conclude, I hope that it has been clear that this is not simply a self-help book. I have given some practical steps which can be taken towards freedom from porn addiction, but none of them should be seen as a 'one size fits all' solution to the problem.

I personally tried many of the steps outlined earlier in my attempts to rid myself of porn on my own. I attempted to break my habit through willpower; several times I wiped my hard drive and determined not to return to porn. Admittedly, one of the steps I've outlined in this book which I didn't use was an accountability partner. I allowed myself to struggle on my own for years because I felt too ashamed to share my problem with anyone else. Needless to say, I was not successful. I started this book with my story, so it is fitting to end it by acknowledging the one who was instrumental in that story.

Every attempt that I made to quit porn only lasted a couple of weeks at best. Even had I succeeded in eliminating porn from my life physically, I would have been unable to rid myself of the temptation, or the feelings of shame which I experienced.

The only person who can take away our guilt and shame is Jesus. There can be no significant and lasting transformation in a person's heart and character unless it is done by Jesus. Jesus lived as a man and experienced all the weakness we experience, with one significant difference: He did not sin. Jesus was tempted in all the ways we are tempted, but because He was fully man and fully God, He was able to resist and remain perfect. Because of this, we are able to come before God through Jesus and receive His mercy and grace.[1]

Mercy and grace are common Christian 'buzzwords'. Simply put, mercy means not getting what we deserve, and grace means getting what we don't deserve (as I mentioned in the previous chapter). We all deserve to be punished for the wrong things that we do. The punishment we all face is death,[2] but through Jesus we receive what we do not deserve – forgiveness. That's mercy.

God doesn't stop there; He also gives us His grace. Through Jesus' death for us we not only gain forgiveness from God, but we are now able to have a personal relationship with Him. When we choose to become followers of Jesus, He removes from us the shame of our sin and replaces it with His own perfection.[3] That's grace.

This can be the reality for all people who struggle with porn addiction. If you're a Christian already, you may be feeling that you can never approach God with what you're facing. I felt that way; I was very aware of the shame of what I was doing, and thought that God wouldn't want anything to do with someone like me. I am thankful every day that the opposite is true! When Jesus set me free from my addiction, He didn't delete the porn from my hard drive; He removed from my heart the desire to look at porn. Over the years since, as I've followed Jesus, He has gradually dealt with the feelings of shame which lingered in me.

As I mentioned in Chapter 5, marriage is not a solution to problems with porn. While it is the proper context in which sexual desire can be fulfilled, it is still all too possible to continue struggling with porn within marriage. I was set free when I was seventeen, and married when I was twenty-five. That was a long journey through which God was working on my heart, well before I even met my wife.

Let me be clear here – what lengthened this process was me. I am convinced that Jesus forgave me of my porn addiction in its entirety – shame and all – the moment He set me free. It was I who held on to the shame all those years. I continued to punish myself in my heart long after Jesus had forgiven me. If you have been forgiven by Jesus for something, it is done. Any time we hold on to the shame of what we've done after we've confessed it to Jesus, we are saying to our souls that we know better than Him.

If you're not a Christian, this same forgiveness is available to you right now. You can receive the mercy and grace of God. Read the Gospels and discover for yourself just who this Jesus is. My recommendation is that you start with the book of Mark. If you want an overview to help you understand what you're reading, check out The Bible Project. You'll find the web address in the Resources section at the end of this book. When you're ready, decide to follow Him and give your life to Him, and you will receive His forgiveness.

Jesus is bigger than porn addiction. He is able to restore people whose lives have been tainted by porn and give them freedom from it. He can do for you what He did for me. Are you prepared to surrender your heart to Jesus so that He can transform you?

Curiosity has killed the intimacy in many lives touched by porn, but if people encounter the risen Jesus and experience true intimacy with Him, renewal can happen in their hearts. It is not too late; nobody has gone too far to be lovingly accepted back by God.

Porn user: Jesus is calling you. Come to Him.

Resources

Books

Carnes, P, *Don't Call It Love: Recovery from Sexual Addiction*, London: Bantam Books, 1992.

Carnes, P, *Out of the Shadows: Understanding Sexual Addiction*, Center City, MN: Hazelden, 2001.

Carnes, P, Delmonico, D L, Griffin, E, with Moriarty, J M, *In the Shadows of the Net: Breaking Free of Compulsive Online Sexual Behavior*, Center City, MN: Hazelden, 2007.

Gross, C, and Harper, J, *Eyes of Integrity: The Porn Pandemic and How It Affects You*, Grand Rapids, MI: Baker Books, 2010.

Loftus, D, *Watching Sex: How Men Really Respond to Pornography*, New York: Thunder's Mouth Press, 2002.

Maltz, W, and Maltz, L, *The Porn Trap: The Essential Guide to Overcoming Problems Caused by Pornography*, London: Harper, 2010.

Rogers, H J, *The Silent War: Ministering to Those Trapped in the Deception of Pornography*, Green Forest, AR: New Leaf Publishing, 2000.

Schaumburg, H, *False Intimacy: Understanding the Struggle of Sexual Addiction*, Colorado Springs, CO: NavPress, 1997.

Schaumburg, H, *Undefiled: Redemption from Sexual Sin, Restoration for Broken Relationships*, Chicago: Moody Publishers, 2009.

Struthers, W M, *Wired for Intimacy: How Pornography Hijacks the Male Brain*, Downers Grove, IL: Inter-Varsity Press, 2009.

Web Resources[1]

The Bible Project (www.thebibleproject.com)
This website is a collection of well-produced videos on a variety of themes and books in the Bible. The videos are helpful and informative, whether you are new to faith or not.

National Center on Sexual Exploitation
(www.endsexualexploitation.org)
This organisation campaigns against sexual exploitation in various areas of society, but particularly pornography. On their site you'll find statistics and research on the effects of porn on individuals and society as a whole.

Fight the New Drug (www.fightthenewdrug.org)

Similarly to NCSE above, Fight the New Drug campaigns to raise awareness of the effects of porn. Among their resources is a web-based course called Fortify designed to help people gain freedom from porn.

XXX Church (www.xxxchurch.com)

XXX Church provide a variety of resources to help battle porn addition. They have produced the accountability software X3 Watch, which you can download from their site.

Covenant Eyes (www.covenanteyes.com)

Covenant Eyes is an alternative accountability software. Their site also has a blog, as well as a library of e-books you can purchase.

Appendix:
Three Key Questions

I'm aware that there may be people reading this book for whom porn addiction has never been a problem. Perhaps there are even some who have never come into contact with porn in any significant way. If this is you, you may be wondering how you can help someone who comes to you asking for help with overcoming porn addiction.

In this short appendix my aim is to provide youth leaders, pastors, parents or friends with some simple questions to ask as a way to begin addressing issues of porn addiction in someone you know. As you'll have discovered in the pages of this book, dealing with porn addiction is not easy, so these questions can only be an entry point for you into conversation. The rest is up to you.

When was your first experience with porn?

This is a question which may not have occurred to many porn users. For some, the first experience will have been so long ago that they have to think hard to remember it. It was only in the process of writing this book that I reflected on my own experience and remembered the first time.

If you can help the person to discover their first exposure to porn, they may then be able to identify the reason why they went back to it. For many people, the reason is simply curiosity. It could equally have been out of loneliness or a desire for intimacy which was not being met elsewhere.

Through uncovering the first experience and the motivation for continued porn use, you may be able to help bring to light some of the core issues in the person's heart which need to be addressed in order to reach freedom from porn addiction.

Do you want to get well?

It never hurts to borrow words from Jesus! In His interaction with the invalid by the pool in John 5, Jesus first asks this question before He heals the man. It may seem like a strange question to ask – why wouldn't he want to get well? Jesus asks the question because when someone has been a certain way for a long time (thirty-eight years, in this case) it can be more comfortable to remain that way than accept change.

With regard to porn use, as with any other addiction, recovery is dependent on there first being a desire to get well. You may have to press them on this. It is possible that their initial 'yes' may be a yes to instant healing, which may not be what God is planning to do for them. If they are going to get well, they have to be prepared to implement discipline and self-control. You'll know if they haven't been honest with you, because not a lot will change until they are truly ready to get well!

What kind of person do you want to be when you're seventy?

This may seem like an odd question at first. After all, how many people realistically have asked themselves this question – particularly young people? That is exactly the purpose of asking it.

So often when dealing with issues of porn addiction, we focus on the immediate – we try to eliminate porn use here and now – or we look back to discover the root issues. Both of those things are valid and good, but it is also helpful to look ahead at what is yet to come.

If you're talking to someone who's trying to quit porn, the likelihood is that they don't want it to be part of their lives by the time they're seventy. It is also likely that they haven't given much thought to how that will become a reality, other than perhaps putting into place certain barriers to stop them accessing porn.

It's good practice for anyone to ask themselves this question, particularly followers of Jesus, because it helps us to identify the gap between who we are now and who we want to become. Through identifying that gap, we can begin to put things into place in our lives which will allow us to become who we want to be. This isn't about changing our personality in a way that is fake; I'm talking about developing godly character over a period of years so that we are conformed more into the likeness of Jesus.

Once they've come up with an answer to the question, you can begin to ask follow-up questions. Their answer could vary from abstract concepts ('I want to be resilient') to specific biblical examples ('I want to be like Joseph') and anything in between. Whatever their answer, your follow-up question will often be the same: 'What can you implement into your life now to help you become more like that?'

Eliminating porn will undoubtedly be on the list of answers, but the aim of these questions is to help the person discover any character faults or weaknesses which lead them to continue using porn. Allow God to redeem those faults, replacing them with godly character, and the desire to look at porn diminishes.

These three questions are just a starting point for conversation. There are no scripts or stock responses for helping people overcome porn addiction, but hopefully this appendix along with the rest of the book will have provided you with some helpful thoughts to guide you as you seek to minister to people caught in the grip of porn.

The goal is always to lead people closer to Jesus. It is an incredible privilege to be used by God to help people escape porn addiction. May God bless you in it!

Notes

1. Porn and Me

[1] Remember the days of MSN Messenger?

[2] Galatians 3:3.

[3] Romans 8:28.

[4] Proverbs 4:23.

[5] 1 Peter 5:8.

[6] James 4:7.

2. Why is Porn a Problem?

[1] C Gross and J Harper, *Eyes of Integrity: The Porn Pandemic and How It Affects You* (Grand Rapids, MI: Baker Books, 2010), p21.

[2] Internet Pornography Statistics, http://pornharmsresearch.com/2012/07/internetpornstatistics/ (accessed 7th July 2017).

[3] 'Cover Exclusive: Jennifer Lawrence Calls Photo Hacking a "Sex Crime"', *Vanity Fair*, November 2014, at https://www.vanityfair.com/hollywood/2014/10/jennifer-lawrence-cover (accessed 18th August 2017).

[4] G M Hald et al., *The APA Handbook of Sexuality and Psychology* (Vol. 2), quoted by K Weir, 'Is Pornography Addictive?', in *Monitor on Psychology* (April 2014), p46.

[5] A Boudreau, 'Mommy Porn Revolution? More Women Seek Erotica, Romance', at http://abcnews.go.com/Entertainment/mommy-porn-

revolution-women-seek-erotica-written-woman/story?id=16182264
(accessed 18th August 2017).

[6] D Fileta, 'Porn Is Not Just a Man's Problem', in *Relevant Magazine*,
https://relevantmagazine.com/life/porn-not-just-mans-problem
(accessed 18th August 2017).

[7] Internet Pornography Statistics,
http://pornharmsresearch.com/2012/07/internetpornstatistics/ (accessed
7th July 2017).

[8] I admit that I don't really know what girls think about during this
stage.

3. Discovering Intimacy

[1] Genesis 2:18, NLT.

[2] K A Mathews, *Genesis 1–11:26 Vol. 1A* (Nashville, TN: Broadman &
Holman Publishers, 1996), p213.

[3] J Donne, *Deuotions upon emergent occasions and seuerall steps in my
sicknes – Meditation XVII* (London: Augustin Mathewes for Thomas
Jones, 1624).

[4] Global Social Media Research Summary, at
http://www.smartinsights.com/social-media-marketing/social-media-
strategy/new-global-social-media-research/ (accessed 10th August
2017).

[5] C Groeschel, *#Struggles: Following Jesus in a Selfie-Centered World*
(Grand Rapids, MI: Zondervan, 2015), p50.

[6] D Kidner, *Genesis: An Introduction and Commentary* (Downers Grove,
IL: Inter-Varsity Press, 1967), p65.

[7] Genesis 2:24.

[8] D Bonhoeffer, *Creation and Fall: A Theological Exposition of Genesis 1–3*
(New York: Touchstone, 1997), p65.

[9] *A Manual For Ministers* (Nottingham: Lifestream Publications, 1993),
p33.

[10] See R Hosie, 'Why Married People Have the Best Sex, According to
Psychotherapist', at http://www.independent.co.uk/life-style/love-
sex/best-sex-married-people-expert-psychotherapist-esther-perel-
relationships-needs-a7862246.html (accessed 11th August 2017).

[11] W M Struthers, *Wired for Intimacy: How Pornography Hijacks the Male
Brain* (Downers Grove, IL: Inter-Varsity Press, 2009), p43.

[12] G G May, *Addiction & Grace* (New York: Harper & Row, 1988), p1.

[13] Psalm 139:13.

[14] Jeremiah 31:3.

[15] John 3:16; 15:13.

[16] Ephesians 1:3-14.

[17] P Scazzero, *Emotionally Healthy Spirituality: It's Impossible to Be Spiritually Mature, while Remaining Emotionally Immature* (Grand Rapids, MI: Zondervan, 2014), p53.

[18] K Shigematsu, *God in My Everything: How an Ancient Rhythm Helps Busy People Enjoy God* (Grand Rapids, MI: Zondervan, 2013), p102.

[19] Oswald Chambers, quoted in G MacDonald, *Building Below the Waterline: Strengthening the Life of a Leader* (Peabody, MA: Hendrickson Publishers, 2013), p12.

[20] Matthew 6:6.

[21] L Morris, *The Gospel According to Matthew* (Grand Rapids, MI: Eerdmans, 1992), p139.

4. Porn and Technology

[1] Arkansas: New Leaf Publishing, 2000.

[2] P Carnes, D L Delmonico, E Griffin and J M Moriarty, *In the Shadows of the Net: Breaking Free of Compulsive Online Sexual Behavior* (Center City, MN: Hazelden, 2007), p6.

[3] Sparks and Honey Culture Forecast, 'Gen Z 2025: The Final Generation', 2016, https://reports.sparksandhoney.com/campaign/generation-z-2025-the-final-generation (accessed 12th September 2017).

[4] Pew Research Centre, http://www.pewinternet.org/2015/04/09/teens-social-media-technology-2015/pi_2015-04-09_teensandtech_06/ (accessed 10th August 2017).

[5] C Moreton, 'Children and the Culture of Pornography: "Boys Will Ask You Every Day until You Say Yes"' at http//www.telegraph.co.uk/women/sex/9828589/Children-and-the-culture-of-pornography-Boys-will-ask-you-every-day-until-you-say-yes.html (accessed 5th June 2017).

5. Porn and Education

[1] 'Not Yet Good Enough: Personal, Social, Health and Economic Education in Schools', Ofsted, 2013, at https://www.gov.uk/government/uploads/system/uploads/attachment _data/file/413178/Not_yet_good_enough_personal__social__health_an d_economic_education_in_schools.pdf (accessed 13th March 2017).

[2] 'PSHE education – an update for school governors – March 17.pdf' at https://www.pshe-association.org.uk/sites/default/files/PSHE%20education%20-%20an%20update%20for%20school%20governors%20-%20March%2017.pdf (accessed 29th July 2017).

[3] I've dealt with that more fully in the chapter 'Sex in the Bible', so I won't address it here.

[4] Dallas Willard, *The Spirit of the Disciplines: Understanding How God Changes Lives* (San Francisco, CA: HarperSanFrancisco, 1991), p176.

[5] John 10:10.

6. Porn and Pastoral Care

[1] John 8:11.

[2] 2 Corinthians 5:21.

7. Porn and the Mind

[1] 2 Corinthians 10:3-5.

[2] A Kinsey, *Sexual Behaviour in the Human Male* (Philadelphia: W B Saunders, 1948), quoted in 'Five Shocking Stats About Men and Sex' on www.psychologytoday.com (accessed 21st June 2017).

[3] Philippians 4:6-9, emphasis mine.

[4] Tony Reinke and John Piper, '12 Questions to Ask Before You Watch "Game of Thrones"', at http://www.desiringgod.org/articles/12-questions-to-ask-before-you-watch-game-of-thrones (accessed 2nd August 2017).

[5] Philippians 4:8.

8. Porn and the Church

[1] Matthew 20:25-28.

[2] John 13:12-17.

[3] 1 Corinthians 1:27.
[4] See Romans 3:23.
[5] Romans 8:1-4.

9. Sex in the Bible

[1] Leviticus 18.
[2] Exodus 22:16.
[3] Deuteronomy 22:20-21.
[4] For example, the Israelites were forbidden from eating pork (Leviticus 11:7; Deuteronomy 14:8), but Peter was told by Jesus in a vision that pork is no longer considered unclean (Acts 10:9-16).
[5] Song of Solomon 2:7; 3:5; 8:4.
[6] Song of Solomon 4:4-7.
[7] Song of Solomon 5:13-16a.
[8] Proverbs 18:22.
[9] 1 Corinthians 5:9-11.
[10] 1 Corinthians 6:12-20.
[11] 1 Corinthians 7:1-9.
[12] Quoted by M Breen, *Multiplying Missional Leaders: From Half-Hearted Followers to a Mobilized Kingdom Force* (Pawleys Island, SC: 3DM, 2012), p9.

10. Masturbation

[1] This is explained in Deuteronomy 25:5-10.
[2] Matthew 15:19; Acts 15:20, 29; Acts 21:25; Romans 13:13; 1 Corinthians 6:18; Galatians 5:19; Ephesians 5:3; Colossians 3:5; 1 Thessalonians 4:3.
[3] 2 Timothy 3:16-17.
[4] Matthew 5:48.
[5] L Morris, *The Gospel According to Matthew* (Grand Rapids, MI: Eerdmans, 1992), p134.
[6] 2 Corinthians 3:18.
[7] Galatians 5:16.
[8] 1 John 1:9; James 5:16.
[9] R T Kendall, *Pigeon Religion: Discern What Is the Holy Spirit and Avoid What Is Not* (Lake Mary, FL: Charisma Media, 2016), p46.

11. Conclusion

[1] Hebrews 4:15-16.
[2] Romans 3:23; 6:23.
[3] 2 Corinthians 5:21.

12. Resources

[1] All websites accurate and up to date as of 23rd September 2017.